PRAYING SCRIPTURAL WONDER WORKING PRAYERS

Kehinde Adelusi

ISBN 979-8-88943-022-3 (paperback)
ISBN 979-8-88943-023-0 (digital)

Copyright © 2023 by Kehinde Adelusi

All rights reserved. No part of this publication may be reproduced, distributed, or transmitted in any form or by any means, including photocopying, recording, or other electronic or mechanical methods without the prior written permission of the publisher. For permission requests, solicit the publisher via the address below.

Christian Faith Publishing
832 Park Avenue
Meadville, PA 16335
www.christianfaithpublishing.com

Printed in the United States of America

Contents

Preface

The Bible instructs believers to pray all manners of prayers and supplications in making their requests known to God. Believers are enjoined to pray without ceasing! The book titled *Praying Scriptural Wonder—Working Prayers* is set out to encourage believers to pray God's word back to God because God upholds all things in the universe by the word of His power. God honors His word when used in prayers. God stands with His word, and His word would never return to Him void. When we use God's word in prayer, God answers our prayers on the integrity of His person and His word. Therefore, let us approach His Throne boldly and with confidence for our God still hears the prayers of His people.

In the season of adversity, when going through the storms of life that come to both great and small; rich and poor, always remember that the word of God works and is able to calm every adverse wind. The word of God is powerful and mighty and is able to pull down every satanic stronghold. To pray effectively, come with true repentance from sin with faith in your heart. Jesus, our loving Lord, is our timely help who is always near and ever willing to hear and answer the cries of His children. Come to Him trusting in the *word of His power*. Place your faith in His word, and you will experience the supernatural operations of God's hand.

Praying in the name of Jesus to God the father quickens answer to our petitions. Jesus gave us the attorney to use His name in prayer. Demons tremble at the mention of His name. Adverse circumstances are turned around at the mention of the highly exalted name of our Lord Jesus Christ. Remember to constantly break the Holy Communion bread and wine, the symbol of His body and blood as ordained by our Lord Jesus Christ. Death is defeated by His blood. We overcome the devil and every situation facing our lives by His blood. Always set aside quality time to fast and pray, just as Jesus revealed to His disciples that some issues in our lives may not be resolved without fasting and prayer.

Faith is a spiritual force through which we receive answers to our prayers. To actually experience the resurrection power of our Lord Jesus Christ in prayer, never negotiate your faith with the devil under any circumstance. In the Epistle of Jude, we are instructed to build up ourselves on our most Holy faith praying in the Holy Ghost. We are also asked to keep ourselves in the love of God looking for the mercy of our Lord Jesus Christ unto eternal life. Prayer is a form of spiritual warfare, and our arsenals include the word of His power, His highly exalted name, His efficacious blood, the power of the Holy Spirit, and our undying faith in God.

Beloved, never forget to come into His presence with thanksgiving in your hearts and also enter His court with praise. Note that there is no deliverance, breakthrough, or healing without thanksgiving. We serve a prayer-answering God who will always honor our faith as we bring our petitions to Him. We receive answers to our prayers out of an overflow of a privileged and robust relationship with our Lord Jesus Christ. Never forget to show Him gratitude whenever your petitions are granted. God is ever faithful, and our faith in Him brings us to victory.

> And it came to pass in those days, that he went out into a mountain to pray, and continued all night in prayer to God. (Luke 6:12)

> And they overcame him by the blood of the lamb, and by the word of their testimony, and they loved not their lives unto the death. (Rev. 12:11)

> Lord, I cry unto thee: make haste unto me; give ear unto my voice, when I cry unto thee. Let my prayers be set forth before thee as incense; and the lifting up of my hands as the evening sacrifice. (Ps. 141:1–2)

That thou wouldest appoint me a set time and remember me! If a man dies, shall he live again? All the days of my appointed time will I wait, till my change come. Thou shall call, and 1 will answer thee: thou wilt have a desire to the work of thine hands. (Job 14:13–15)

Jesus answered and said unto them, Verily I say unto you, if ye have faith, and doubt not, ye shall not only do this which is done to the fig tree, but also if ye shall say unto this mountain, be thou removed, and be thou cast into the sea; it shall be done. And all things, whatsoever ye shall ask in prayer, believing, ye shall receive. (Matt. 21:21–22)

And in that day ye shall ask me nothing. Verily, verily, I say unto you, Whatsoever ye shall ask the Father in my name, he will give it you. Hitherto have ye asked nothing in my name: ask, and ye shall receive that your joy may be full. (John 16:23–24)

Giving Thanks to God

Psalm 34

1. I will bless the Lord at all times: His praise shall continually be in my mouth.
2. My soul shall make her boast in the Lord: the humble shall hear thereof and be glad.
3. O, magnify the Lord with me, and let us exalt His name together.
4. I sought the Lord, and He heard me and delivered me from all my fears.
5. They looked unto Him and were lightened: and their faces were not ashamed.
6. This poor man cried, and the Lord heard him and saved him out of all his troubles.
7. The angel of the Lord encamped round about them that fear Him and delivered them.
8. O, taste and see that the Lord is good: blessed is the man that trusted in Him.
9. O, fear the Lord, ye His saints: for there is no want to them that fear Him.
10. The young lions do lack and suffer hunger: but they that seek the Lord shall not want any good thing.

Attributes of God

The Lord is good, and His mercies endure forever.

He is Jehovah Jireh; the Waymaker; the Great Provider;

the God of all Possibilities;

the God Almighty who can reverse the irreversible;

the Great I Am;

the Faithful and Merciful High Priest;

the only Covenant Keeper;

the Yoke Breaker, and

the Faithful Creator;

the Eternal, Immortal, Invincible, the Only Wise God;

the God that performs all things for me.

To You, Lord, be all the glory, all the honor, and adoration forevermore.

I give thanks to God who has always caused me to triumph in Christ and has manifested His knowledge in me in every place (2 Cor. 2:14).

Prayer of Consecration

Who shall ascend into the hill of the Lord? Or who shall stand in his holy place? He that has clean hands, and a pure heart, who has not lifted up his soul unto vanity, nor sworn deceitfully. (Ps. 24:3–4)

If I regard iniquity in my heart, the Lord will not hear me. (Ps. 66:18)

In that day there shall be a fountain opened to the house of David and to the inhabitants of Jerusalem for sin and for uncleanness. (Zech. 13:1)

> Search me, O, God, and know my heart:
> try me and know my thoughts: And see if there
> be any wicked way in me and lead me in the way
> everlasting. (Ps. 139:23–24)

1. Father God, I thank you for the privilege of knowing you as my Lord and Savior. Thank you for accepting me in the beloved. Thank you for being the only prayer-answering God. Thank you for the blood of the redemption that granted me access into your presence morning, noon, and night, in Jesus' name (Ps. 55:17).

2. Father God, I receive the Spirit of grace and supplication to pray aright, in Jesus' name. I ask and receive the supply of the Spirit of our Lord Jesus Christ as I pray, in Jesus' name. Lord Jesus, I make a demand on the blood and the water that flows from your pierced sides to cleanse me from all my sins and filths, in Jesus' name (John 19:34).

3. Dear Lord, I ask in the name of Jesus that You cleanse and sanctify me with the water of Your word. Remove every spot, wrinkle, and blemish from my life with Your blood, in Jesus' name (Eph. 5:26–27).

4. Father God, let Your Holy Spirit quicken me out of all my trespasses and sins. Deliver me from the operations of the prince of the power of the air that works disobedience in me, in Jesus' name (Eph. 2:1–2).

5. Lord Jesus, help me to walk worthy of God who hath called me into His Kingdom and glory, in Jesus' name. May the devil not hinder or block my way, in Jesus' name (1 Thes. 2:12, 18).

6. Dear Lord, perfect that which is lacking in my faith, in Jesus' name. Make me increase and abound in love toward others, establish my heart unblameable in holiness before God, even our father at the coming of our Lord Jesus Christ with all the saints, in Jesus' name (1 Thes. 3:10, 12, 13).

7. Lord Jesus, quicken me by Your spirit in my inner man so that I will not give room/place to the devil in any area of my life, in Jesus' name (Eph. 4:27).

8. Father God, I receive the supply of the spirit of our Lord Jesus Christ all through this day, week, month, year, and all my days to keep me going on the path of truth and righteousness, in Jesus' mighty name (Phil. 1:19).

9. Father God, help me to abstain from all sexual sins and fleshly lust, in Jesus' name. (1 Thes. 4:3, 5). Cleanse and purify my thoughts always, in Jesus' name.

10. Father God, I ask that You deliver me from all sinful lifestyles and let them not have dominion over me, in Jesus' name (Rom. 6:12).

11. Father Lord, help me to be sober, watchful, and full of faith, love, and hope as I await Your second coming, in Jesus' name (1 Thes. 5:8).

12. Lord Jesus, strengthen me to always wrestle in prayer for all my concerns/issues so that I may stand firm in all the will of God mature and fully assured, in Jesus' name (Col. 4:12).

13. Dear Lord, help me to forget those things which are behind (past failures/past victory). Help me to reach forth unto those things which are before, in Jesus' name (Phil. 3:13).

14. Father Lord, I ask that my eyes of understanding be enlightened and that I may know what the hope of Your calling is and what the riches of the glory of my inheritance in the saints are and what is the exceeding greatness of Your power to me who believes in Your resurrection power, in Jesus' name (Eph. 1:18–19).

15. Father Lord, help me to show myself a pattern of good works in doctrine, showing incorruptness, gravity, sincerity, and sound speech that cannot be condemned, in Jesus' name (Titus 2:7–8).

16. Father in the mighty name of Jesus, I acknowledge every good thing, which is in me in Christ Jesus. Let the communication of my faith become effectual, in Jesus' name (Philem. 1:6).

17. Lord Jesus, help me to learn to maintain good works so that my life will not be unfruitful, in Jesus' name (Titus 3:14).

18. Lord Jesus, may I never deny You in works, actions, and deeds as a Christian, in Jesus' name (Titus 1:16).

19. May the Father of our Lord Jesus count me worthy of His calling and fulfill all the good pleasure of His goodness and work of faith with power in me. May the name of our Lord Jesus

Christ be glorified in me and I in Him according to the grace of our God and the Lord Jesus Christ, in Jesus' name (2 Thes. 1:11–12).

20. May the Lord Jesus Christ Himself and God, even our Father, who loved me and has given me everlasting consolation and good hope through grace, comfort my heart and establish me in every good word and work, in Jesus' name (2 Thess. 2:16–17).

21. May the Lord God direct my heart unto the love of God and unto the patient waiting for Christ, in Jesus' name (2 Thes. 3:5).

22. Lord Jesus, help me to war good warfare holding faith and good conscience so that I will not make a shipwreck of my Christian faith, in Jesus' name (1 Tim. 1:18–19).

23. Father Lord, I pray that from today henceforth that the will/ mind of the Lord shall be made known and clear to me on all issues of my life, in Jesus' name (Lev. 24:12).

24. Father Lord, help me by Your spirit not to sin against the Holy Spirit in any area of my life, in Jesus' name (Mk. 3:29).

25. Father Lord, I ask that You free me from secret faults, in Jesus' name. Deliver me from presumptuous sins. Let them not have dominion over me, in Jesus' name (Ps. 19:12–13).

26. Father God, I ask that You deliver me from lying spirit, stealing, and spirit of laziness, in Jesus' name (Eph. 4:25–29).

27. Dear God, help me to overcome all the irritations of life, and give me to eat of the tree of life that is in the midst of the paradise of God, in Jesus' name (Rev. 2:7).

28. Lord Jesus, help me not to lose my place with You in eternity and in destiny, in Jesus' name. May I remain relevant in Your program in all seasons of my life, in Jesus' name (Matt. 19:28).

29. Father God, help me to be sober and watchful so that Your second coming does not catch me unaware, in Jesus' name (Matt. 24:42–43).

30. Father Lord, as I make efforts to enter through the narrow door, be thou my strength and guide me in the way, in Jesus' mighty name (Lk. 13:24).

31. Dear Lord, help me to live my life according to Your plan and purpose, in Jesus' mighty name (Exod. 25:40).

32. Father Lord, I humble myself before You today that You might lift me up and honor my faith in You, in Jesus' name (Lk. 14:11).

33. Lord Jesus, anoint me afresh and give me oil in my lamp; keep me burning till I see You in glory, in Jesus' name (Exod. 27:20).

34. Lord Jesus, You are the light of the world. Cause me to walk before You in the light of the living. Help me to keep believing in the light. Flood my life with Your light. Let darkness not have any hiding place in my life and borders, in Jesus' name (John 12:35, 46).

35. Lord Jesus, help me to continue to abide in You so that when You appear in Your glory, I will be confident and will not be ashamed. Make me a true reflection of Your glory, in Jesus' name (1 John 2:28).

36. Have mercy upon me, O, Lord! Do not replace me with stones. Let me remain relevant in Your program all the days of my life, in Jesus' name (Matt. 3:9).

37. Father God, You are the giver of all good gifts. Every good gift You have given to me shall not be taken or given to another under any guise. God's gift in my life shall not be corrupted, in Jesus' name (Lk. 11:13).

38. Lord Jesus, please fill me with the Holy Spirit to overflow in the mighty name of Jesus (Acts 7:55). Holy Spirit be my leader and mentor in the journey of life, in Jesus' name.

39. Lord Jesus, I pray that You establish my heart with grace. Make my heart perfect in every good work and to always do Your will. Work in me that which is well pleasing in Your sight through Jesus Christ, in Jesus' name (Heb. 13:9, 21).

40. Holy Spirit dear, please empower me to be a worthy witness of the gospel of grace. Pour Your Holy Spirit upon me, in Jesus' name (Acts 2:32–33).

41. Father God, please let a time of refreshing come upon me from the presence of the Lord, in Jesus' name. Make me fruitful in every area of my life, in Jesus' mighty name (Acts 3:19).

42. Lord Jesus, give me the heart to always obey You in all things. Let me be blessed always and make me a channel of blessing always, in Jesus' name (Gen. 22:18).

43. Father God, help me to contend for the faith that was once delivered unto the saints and me. Empower me to always keep myself in the love of God, in Jesus' name (Jude 3:21).

44. Dear Lord, give me the grace to always take You at Your word in every circumstance of my life, in Jesus' name (Lk. 5:5). Help me, Lord, never to reject Your counsel for my life in any situation and in any circumstance of my life, in Jesus' name.

45. Lord Jesus, help me to walk faithfully with You every day of my life, in Jesus' name (Gen. 5:24). Help me to walk in love as Christ has loved me and has given Himself as an offering and sacrifice to God for a sweet-smelling savor, in Jesus' name. May my life be filled with Your sweet-smelling fragrance, in Jesus' name (Eph. 5:2).

CHAPTER 2

Spiritual Warfare

Taking authority over the operations of the powers of darkness

For we wrestle not against flesh and blood, but against principalities, against powers, Against the rulers of the darkness of this world, against spiritual wickedness in high places. (Eph. 6:12)

Who hath delivered us from the power of darkness, and hath translated us into the kingdom of his dear son in whom we have redemption through his blood, even the forgiveness of sins. (Col. 1:13)

> And they overcame him by the blood of the Lamb, and by the word of their testimony; and they loved not their lives unto the death. (Rev. 12:11)

> And the earth helped the woman, and the earth opened her mouth, and swallowed up the flood which the dragon cast out of his mouth. (Rev. 12:16)

> Have respect unto the covenant: For the dark places of the earth are full of the habitation of cruelty. (Ps. 74:20)

1. *Father, in the mighty name of Jesus, I come by the blood of the new and the living way. I come by the blood of the eternal covenant.* I take authority over every principality, power, spiritual wickedness in high places, and all ground-level demons working against me, in Jesus' name. I blot out by the blood of Jesus Christ every handwriting of ordinances written against me that is contrary to Your good plans and purpose for my life, in Jesus' name. I nail them to the cross of Calvary, in Jesus' name (Col. 2:14).

2. *It is written, "Associate yourselves, O, ye people, and ye shall be broken in pieces*; and give ear, all ye of far countries: gird yourselves, and ye shall be broken in pieces; gird yourselves, and ye shall be broken in pieces. Take counsel together, and it shall come to nought; speak the word, and it shall not stand for God is with us" (Isa. 8:9–10). Therefore, I decree no weapon fashioned against me shall prosper, in Jesus' name. No satanic verdict, sentence, curses, or utterances shall have effect over any area of my life, in Jesus' name.

3. Father Lord, in the name that is above every other name, Jesus Christ, I command every power of wickedness and opposition working and operating against my destiny, family, ministry, business, and career to bow today, in Jesus' unfailing name (Phil. 2:9–10).

4. Father, in the mighty name of Jesus, deliver me from every evil work and preserve me unto Your heavenly kingdom. To You be the glory forever and ever, in Jesus' name (11 Tim. 4:18).

5. Lord Jesus, I come against all lying and deceiving spirits that are set to deceive me out of God's plan and purpose for my life, family, ministry, business, and career, in Jesus' mighty name (2 Chron. 18:21).

6. My Father and my God, stretch forth Your mighty hand against the wrath of my enemies that they may know that the earth is the Lord's and the fullness thereof, in Jesus' mighty name (Exod. 9:29).

7. In the mighty name of Jesus, any human being or demonic being that has taken an oath not to eat or drink until they have destroyed my life, family, ministry, and career or that has entered a covenant with the devil to work against my life, family, ministry, and business, let them be accursed, and let them be roasted in the fire of the God of the consuming fire, in Jesus' name (Acts 23:21).

8. Lord Jesus, please deliver me from all the activities of dream killers and glory hijackers, in Jesus' name (Gen. 37:5–8).

9. Father, in the mighty name of Jesus, I come against the fulfillment of every form of negative prophecies, covenants, satanic verdicts, sentences, evil wishes, and demonic utterances that may want to influence my destiny/life and my generation negatively, in Jesus' name (Gen. 16:12).

10. Father Lord, in the name that is above every other name, Jesus Christ, I evoke the spirit of judgment and of fire against the wicked who have determined to steal, kill, and destroy my life, family, ministry, business, and career, and in all my borders, in Jesus' mighty name (Isa. 4:4).

11. Father God, contend against all the forces of darkness contending and warring against my glorious destiny, family, ministry, business, and career, in Jesus' name (Isa. 41:12).

12. I decree destruction and disaster on every serpentine spirit, household witchcraft, envious witchcraft, household wickedness, familiar spirit, ancestral forces, generational curses, spells,

jinx, marine altars, and satanic agents assigned to work against my destiny/life and the call of God upon my life. I come against all their evil schemes and machinations, in Jesus' name.

13. I decree disaster upon any satanic personality that burns incense to any god on any evil altar or engages in divination and enchantments against any area of my life, in Jesus' mighty name. Every force from hell that is set to destroy the tree of my life and its fruit, I bring upon them the vengeance of the Almighty God, in Jesus' name (Jer. 11:18–20).

14. Father, in the mighty name of our Lord Jesus Christ, I declare that every evil counsel taken against my destiny and every plan taken to vex my mind and spirit on any evil altar in the heavenlies, on the earth, under the earth, or in the waters shall not stand neither shall it come to pass, in Jesus' mighty name (Isa. 7:5–7).

15. I decree in the name that is above every other name, Jesus Christ, the Resurrected Lord, both seen and unseen forces of darkness and satanic altars of my father's house that have been mobilized to fight against my destiny and all that concerns me from the heavenlies, on the earth, under the earth, and in the waters be roasted by the fire of the Consuming Fire, in Jesus' name.

16. Lord Jesus, Your word says You will cause wasters of life and destiny to depart from me and my family. Let God arise now against every familiar spirit, ancestral force, household witchcraft, serpentine spirit, strongman/strongwoman of darkness, marine and water spirits, and spirit of pharaoh and violence, I command all these agents of darkness to depart from all my borders, in Jesus' name. I raise the standard of the Holy Ghost against all wasters assigned against my glorious destiny, in Jesus Christ. I paralyzed all Your activities against me in all frontiers of my life, in Jesus' name (Isa. 49:17–19; 59:19).

17. Every repressive, suppressive, and oppressive force seen and unseen that is assigned to waste my honest efforts and glorious destiny, I hereby decree destruction by the fire of the Holy Spirit upon You all, in Jesus' name. Be consumed to ashes, in Jesus' name.

18. Father Lord, I ask that the whirlwind of the Holy Ghost scatter to desolation every force of hell assigned against my life and God-given destiny, in Jesus' name (Isa. 41:16).

19. Father Lord, in the name that is above every other name, Jesus Christ, the Resurrected Lord, I decree trouble and anguish upon every enemy of my soul who is after my life and wellbeing to destroy. In as much as they have stretched out their hands against the Lord and His anointed, and because they have strengthened themselves against the Almighty, the Host of Heaven shall prevail against them, and their candles shall be put out. Their roots shall be dried up beneath, and above, their branches shall be cut off. The light of the wicked shall be put out completely, and the spark of their fire shall not shine anymore, in Jesus' mighty name (Job 18:5, 6, 16).

20. I declare in the name that is above all other names Jesus Christ, the Resurrected Lord, the Good Lord will keep my soul, and every plan of the enemy to take away my life prematurely in this season is frustrated, in Jesus' mighty name. The Good Lord shall satisfy me with long life and good health, and I shall fulfill my days, in Jesus' name (Job 5:26).

21. I declare that as I go out today, the steadfast love of God shall abide with me, His goodness and mercy shall overtake me, and everyone connected to me. Men and women from all nations shall compete to favor me everywhere I go in the precious name of our Lord Jesus Christ.

22. Father Lord, in the mighty name of Jesus, I declare that I shall go out with joy today, and I shall be led forth with peace. Mountains of challenges and hills of oppositions shall break forth before me into singing, and all the trees of the field shall clap their hands. Situations and people will compete to celebrate with me. Instead of thorns shall come up the fir tree and instead of brier shall come up the myrtle tree. I shall receive God's all-around blessings in all circumstances of life, in Jesus' name (Isa. 55:12–13).

23. Father Lord, I receive a new sharp threshing instrument having teeth/mantle; I thresh and tackle the mountains of oppositions;

and I beat them small; I make the hills of hindrances and stagnancy, failure, and defeat as chaff, in Jesus' name (Isa. 41:15).

24. Father Lord, I decree that every long-standing issue in my life, family, ministry, business, and career that has caused me so much pain, tears, and sorrow is receiving a divine query right now, in Jesus' name. I command such issues to dry up, in Jesus' name. I command the root of that problem to loosen its grip over me right now, in Jesus' name. Every evil tree in my foundation be rooted up, in Jesus' name (Isa. 40:24).

25. I declare in the name above all other names, that I am seated with Christ in heavenly places. Far above all principality, and power, and might, and dominion, in the mighty name of Jesus (Eph. 1:20–21).

26. It is written, "Behold, I will make thee a new sharp threshing instrument having teeth: thou shall thresh the mountains, and beat them small, and shall make the hills as chaff" (Isa. 41:15). Father, in the mighty name of Jesus, I receive the instrument of warfare, and I destroy all oppositions and barriers to my breakthrough and destiny, in Jesus' name.

CHAPTER 3

Fasting/Waiting upon the Lord in Prayer

For we have not a high priest which cannot be touched with the feeling of our infirmities; but was in all points tempted like as we are, yet without sin. Let us therefore come boldly unto the throne of grace, that we may obtain mercy, and find grace to help in time of need. (Heb. 4:15–16)

The LORD is good unto them that wait for him, To the soul that seeketh him. It is good that a man should both hope and quietly Wait for the salvation of the Lord. (Lam. 3:25–26)

Even the youths shall faint and be weary, and the young men shall utterly fall: but they that

wait upon the Lord shall renew their strength;
they shall mount up with wings as eagles; they
shall run, and not be weary; and they shall walk,
and not faint. (Isa. 40:30–31)

1. Lord Jesus, I pray today for a divine encounter that will terminate sorrow, stress, sweat, curses, spells, jinx, and struggles in every area of my life, family, career and ministry, finance, career, and health, in Jesus' name (Gen. 32:28).

2. It is written, *"And it came to pass in those days, that he went out into a mountain to pray, and continued all night in prayer to God"* *(Lk. 6:12)*. Father Lord, grant me the grace to maintain a cordial relationship with You so that my prayers to You may continue to produce wonders to the glory of Your name, in Jesus' name.

3. *It is written, "For unto us a child is born, unto us a son is given, and the government shall be upon his shoulder: and his name shall be called Wonderful, Counselor, The mighty God, The everlasting Father, The Prince of Peace" (Isa. 9:6).* Father Lord, I accept Your offer of salvation through Jesus Christ, my Lord today, in Jesus' name. Lord, receive me and forgive me as I (re)dedicate my life to You today, in Jesus' name. Grant me the grace to always obey you in all areas of my life, in Jesus' name. Help me, Lord, to fulfill Your divine purpose for my life, in Jesus' mighty name.

4. Dear God, please make Your face shine upon me, in Jesus' name. Make me the focus of Your attention; look in my direction and help me. Let the light of Your countenance be upon me always. Flood my life with light. In Your light will I see light, and no darkness shall be able to overtake me, in Jesus' name.

5. Oh, Lord, I know that the way of man is not in Himself. It is not in man that walketh to direct His steps. Oh, Lord! Order my step alright. Teach me the way to go and profit, in Jesus' name (Jer. 10:23; Ps. 37).

6. Dear Lord, make me a fenced brazen wall, and they shall fight me, and they shall not prevail against me. For the Lord is with me to save and deliver me (Jer. 15:20). God will deliver us out

of the hand of the wicked and will redeem us out of the hand of the terrible, in Jesus' mighty name (Jer. 15:21).

7. Lord Jesus, rid me and deliver me from the hand of strange children (Ps. 144:11). May my sons be as plants that have grown up in their youth; make my daughters cornerstones polished after the similitude of a palace. Lord, make them polished pillars of Your kingdom, in Jesus' name (Ps. 144:12).

8. Dear Lord God, please send Your angel ahead of me to guard me along the way and to bring me to the place You have prepared for me, in Jesus' name. Bless my bread and water and take sickness from among us, in Jesus' name (Exod. 23:20–26).

9. In the mighty name of Jesus, every force working against the perfect will of God for my life be frustrated and paralyzed now, in Jesus' name (Acts 4:6–12). Lord, restore me to perfect fellowship with You, in Jesus' name.

10. Dear Lord Jesus, please bear me on eagle's wings and cause me to soar above every difficulty in life, in Jesus' name (Exod. 19:4).

11. Father, in the name of Jesus, let Your power that delivers rescue me from all afflictions and all operations of the powers of darkness, in Jesus' name (Lk. 8:46).

12. Father, in Jesus' name, I ask that You disappoint the devices of the crafty/the wicked in my life and family so that their hands cannot perform their enterprise, in Jesus' mighty name. (Job 5:12).

CHAPTER 4

The Battle in Our Heart

For out of the heart proceed evil thoughts, murders, adulteries, fornications, thefts, false witness, blasphemies: These are the things which defile a man. (Matt. 15:19–20)

For from within, out of the heart of men, proceed evil thoughts, adulteries, fornications, murders, thefts, covetousness, wickedness, deceit, lasciviousness, an evil eye, blasphemy, pride, foolishness: All these evil things come from within, and defile the man. (Mk 7:21–23)

Wherefore gird up the loins of your mind be sober. (1 Pet. 1:13)

Fear thou not; for I am thy God: I am with thee be not dismayed; for I am thy God: I will strengthen thee; yea, I will help thee; yea, I will uphold thee with the right hand of my righteousness. (Isa. 41:10)

Thou wilt keep him in perfect peace, whose mind is stayed on thee: because he trusted in thee. (Isa. 26:3)

Be careful for nothing; but in everything by prayer and supplication with thanksgiving let your requests be made known unto God. And the peace of God, which passes all understanding, shall keep your hearts and minds through Christ Jesus. (Phil. 4:6–7)

Praying against anxious thoughts, negative thoughts, depressive thoughts, suicidal thoughts, ideations, lustful thoughts, addiction to drugs, gambling, and untimely death.

1. In the name that is above every other name, Jesus Christ, the Resurrected Lord, I choose joy over sorrow and anxious thoughts. I will not be anxious over any matter or situation, but by prayer and supplication with thanksgiving, I shall make my request known to God. I declare that the peace of God shall flood my heart and mind through Jesus Christ, my Lord. I shall think and meditate over things that are true, honest, just, and of good report (Phil. 4:6–7). I shall with joy draw out of the well of salvation, in Jesus' name.

2. In the name that is above all other names, Jesus Christ, the Resurrected Lord, I cast down imaginations and every high thing that exalts itself against the knowledge of God in my life, and I bring into captivity every thought to the obedience of Christ, in Jesus' name (2 Cor. 10:5).

3. Father Lord, I receive power to keep my heart with all diligence, for out of it springs the issues of life, in Jesus' name (Prov. 4:23).

4. Father Lord, strengthen my heart, reasoning, and imagination so that I do not give any room to the devil in my heart to entertain lustful thoughts, negative thoughts, depressive thoughts, suicide thoughts, and thought of addiction to substance use (cocaine, heroin, weed, tobacco, alcohol), in Jesus' name (Eph. 4:27).

5. I declare that God has delivered me from the powers of darkness, and I have been translated into the kingdom of His only begotten son Jesus Christ, in Jesus' name (Col. 1:13). Father Lord, I ask that You deliver me from the prison of addiction, lust, evil thoughts, and imagination, in Jesus' name. Show me mercy Lord, in Jesus' name.

6. I declare in the name that is above all other names, Jesus Christ the Resurrected Lord, that in this season, the Good Lord will keep my soul, and every plan of the enemy to take away my life prematurely is frustrated, in Jesus' name. The Good Lord shall satisfy me with long life and good health, in Jesus' name (Job 5:26).

7. In the mighty name of Jesus, I declare that the Good Lord has ransomed my soul and has delivered me from going down into the pit. God has redeemed me from the power of the grave, in the mighty name of Jesus (Job 33:24).

8. I declare in the mighty name of Jesus; I shall not die but live to declare the goodness and the wonders of God in the land of the living, in Jesus' name (Ps. 118:17). I shall live to my good old age, in Jesus' name.

9. I come by the blood of the new and the living way. I come by the blood of the eternal covenant. I declare that the Spirit of God made me and that the breath of the Almighty gave me life. Therefore, any flesh and blood or spirit being that did not give me life is not permitted to terminate my life prematurely, in Jesus' name (Job 33:3).

10. Father Lord, I declare that I have been crucified with Christ; it is no longer I who live, but Christ lives in me, in Jesus' name (Gal. 2:20).

11. Father Lord, I boldly declare that I have eaten the flesh of Jesus, and I have drunk His blood I have the life of God in me. I have eternal life, in Jesus' name (1 John 5:7–8).

12. In the mighty name of Jesus, I annul every covenant with death and every agreement reached by anyone or demonic being over my life shall not stand, in Jesus' name (Isa. 28:15–18).

13. Father Lord, I declare boldly that the power that raised Jesus from the grave has ransomed me from the power of the grave and evil circumstance and untimely death, in Jesus' name (Hos. 13:14).

14. To appoint unto them that mourn in Zion, to give unto them beauty for ashes, the oil of joy for mourning, the garment of praise for the spirit of heaviness, in Jesus' name (Isa. 61:3). Therefore, when the enemy shall come in like a flood of evil, depressive, suicidal thoughts, the Holy Ghost shall raise a standard against them, in Jesus' name (Isa. 59:19).

15. Father Lord, I declare that Your good thoughts concerning my life be established upon me in this season of my life, in Jesus' name. The thought of peace and a glorious expectation are established upon me, in Jesus' name. Every contrary and negative thought shall not find fulfillment in any area of my life, in Jesus' name (Jer. 29:11).

16. Father Lord, even when I seek to kill myself, cause Your glorious light and life to penetrate my miserable heart and my bitter soul, in Jesus' name (Job 3:20–21).

17. It is written, "And they overcame him by the blood of the Lamb, and by the word of their testimony; and they loved not their lives unto death." Therefore, in the mighty name of Jesus Christ, the Resurrected Lord, and by the reason of the blood that was shed for me at Calvary, I plead the blood of Jesus over my life and family against death and all the operations of the forces of the enemy working against my life, in Jesus' name (Rev. 12:11).

18. It is written, "Finally, brethren, whatsoever things are true, whatsoever things are honest, whatsoever things are just, whatsoever things are pure, whatsoever things are lovely, whatsoever things are of good report; if there be any virtue, and if there be any

praise, think on these things. Those things, which ye have both learned and received, and heard, and seen in me, do: and the God of peace shall be with you" (Phil. 4:8–9). Father God, I ask that You free me from the trap of suicide thoughts and thoughts of masturbation, prostitution, pornography, drug addictions, lesbianism, homosexualism, gay, pedophile, and all manner of sexual lusts, in Jesus' name. I speak life and peace over my life, and I reject death, in Jesus' name (Prov. 18:21).

19. As the Good Lord lives, I shall fulfill the numbers of my days, and I shall come to my grave in a full age like as a shock of corn comes in its season, in Jesus' mighty name (Job 5:26).

20. Father Lord, thank You for granting me life and favor, and thy visitation shall continue to preserve my spirit, soul, and body, in Jesus' name (Job 10:12).

Praying for a Life Partner

Seek ye out of the book of the LORD, and read: no one of these shall fail, none shall want her mate: for my mouth, it hath commanded, and his spirit it hath gathered them. (Isa. 34:16)

And the LORD God said, it is not good that man should be alone; I will make him an help meet for him. (Gen. 2:18)

And the LORD God caused a deep sleep to fall upon Adam, and he slept: and he took one of his ribs, and closed up the flesh instead thereof, and the rib, which the LORD God had taken from man, made he a woman, and brought her unto the man. And Adam said, this is now bone of my bone, and flesh of my flesh: she shall

be called Woman, because she was taken out of
Man. (Gen. 2:21–23)

Therefore, shall a man leave his father and
mother, and shall cleave unto his wife: and they
shall be one flesh. (Gen. 2:24)

1. Father Lord, the book of the Lord says, "No one of these shall fail, none shall want her mate for the mouth of the Lord has commanded and his spirit has gathered them." Therefore, in the name that is above all other names, Jesus Christ the Resurrected Lord, I ask that the Holy Spirit divinely connect me with my life partner now, in Jesus' mighty name (Isa. 34:16).

2. Father Lord, in the mighty name of Jesus, I receive the divine favor that I need to be divinely connected to my life partner because Your word says He who finds a wife finds a good thing and has obtained favor from the Lord (Prov. 18:22). Father Lord, grant me the favor for marital settlement and fruitfulness, in Jesus' name.

3. I receive a God-fearing, considerate, and compassionate wife, in Jesus' mighty name.

4. Father Lord, in the name that is above all other names, Jesus Christ, just as Esther obtained favor in the sight of all that looked upon her and the king loved her above all women, let me be the preferred choice of the man You have prepared me for and that You have ordained for my life, in Jesus' mighty name (Esth. 2:15–17).

5. In the mighty name of our Lord Jesus Christ, every force of darkness working against God's perfect will for my life be frustrated and paralyzed now, in Jesus' name. I take authority over every familiar spirit, household witchcraft, envious witchcraft, generational curses, premature death, infirmities, barrenness, ancestral spirit/altars, and serpentine spirit operations. I stop them from working against my marital settlement, in Jesus' mighty name. I stop the influence of these spirits and altars from breaking up my relationship, in Jesus' name. I arrest every spirit husband/

wife working against my marital settlement and fruitfulness. I release the judgment of fire upon all of them, in Jesus' name.

6. I receive a God-fearing, loving, and caring husband, in Jesus' mighty name.

7. It is written, "In the day that thy walls are to be built, in that day shall the decree be far removed" (Micah 7:11). Father Lord, I ask that You remove every wall of Jericho and every Red Sea that may be hindering our marital destiny, in Jesus' name. I come against anti-marriage spells, jinx, and demonic dreams, in Jesus' name. I take authority over ancestral curses fighting my marital destiny and marital settlement, in Jesus' mighty name. Be frustrated and terminated, in Jesus' mighty name.

8. Lord Jesus, lead me to my divine helper that is suitable for me as You did for Adam in the Garden of Eden, in Jesus' name (Gen. 2:20).

9. It is written, "He brought me to the banqueting house, and his banner over me was his love" (Song of Sol. 2:4). Lord Jesus, I ask that You bring us to the banqueting house and let Your love be the banner over our lives, in Jesus' name.

10. Father Lord, by terrible things in righteousness, locate and divinely connect me to the bone of my bone and to the flesh of my flesh, in Jesus' name. May I not marry wrongly, O Lord, in Jesus' name (Ps. 65:5; Gen. 2:22–23). I come against arrows of rejection and disfavor, in Jesus' name. Lord Jesus, let me find favor in the eyes of all my in-laws. Let me be acceptable to the family, in Jesus' name.

Praying for Your Spouse for a Happy Marriage

That their hearts may be encouraged, being knit together in love, and attaining to all riches of the full assurance of understanding, to the knowledge of the mystery of God, both of the Father and of Christ. (Col. 2:2)

Wives, submit yourself unto your own husbands as unto the Lord. For the husband is the head of the wife, even as Christ is the head of the church: and he is the savior of the body. (Eph. 5:22–23)

Husbands, love your wives, even as Christ also loved the church, and gave himself for it; that he might sanctify and cleanse it with the washing of water by the word... For this, cause shall a man leave his father and mother, and shall be joined unto his wife, and the two shall be one flesh. (Eph. 5:25–33)

She is your companion and wife by covenant so be faithful. Therefore, take heed to your spirit, and let no one deal treacherously against the wife of his youth. (Mal. 2:14–15)

1. Father God, I ask in the mighty name of Jesus that You empower my man/husband with the ability to leave, cleave, and weave with me in matrimony according to Your word in Genesis 2:24, in Jesus' name.
2. Father Lord, empower me to love, nourish, and cherish my wife as my own body as Christ loves the Church and sacrificed His life for her according to the scriptures in Ephesians 5:26–31, in Jesus' mighty name.
3. Father Lord, I ask that You grant me the grace to be submissive to my husband in all things according to the scriptures in Ephesians 5:22–24 in the mighty name of Jesus.
4. Father God, I ask that You empower me to live in peace with my spouse. May the God of love and peace reign in our lives and home, in Jesus' name. Lord, I ask that You make us of one mind and help us to live in peace with each other for life, in Jesus' name (2 Cor. 13:11).
5. Father God, I ask that You endow me with the wisdom to build my house as a wise woman in the mighty name of Jesus (Prov. 14:1).
6. Father God, I ask that You empower me with wealth/resources so that I will be able to meet the needs of my wife and family as the head of the wife/ home, in Jesus' name.

7. It is written, "Can two walk together, except they agreed?" (Amos 3:3). Father Lord, we receive the spirit of agreement and understanding in our marriage, in Jesus' name. Father, help us to keep the unity of the spirit in our lives and home. Help us to endeavor to keep the unity of the spirit in the bond of peace. Lord God, give us peace by all means, in Jesus' name. We reject the operations of every demonic spirit that promotes conflict, discord, disagreement, and misunderstanding in our home and marriage, in Jesus' name.

8. Father Lord, I take authority over the spirit of argument, hatred, malice, bitterness, strife, unforgiveness, jealousy, envy, pride, infidelity, fleshly lust/immorality, sexual perversion, and covetousness in our lives, in Jesus' name. I declare that none of these anti-marriage demons assigned against our lives/marriage shall prosper, in Jesus' mighty name. They shall not have a place in our lives/home/marriage, in Jesus' name.

9. Father God, I ask that You empower us by Your spirit not to engage in the works of the flesh namely: adultery, fornication, lasciviousness, uncleanness, witchcraft, idolatry, murders, drunkenness, pool-betting, and reveling, in Jesus' mighty name. Help us to crucify the flesh with its affections, in Jesus' name (Gal. 5:19, 24).

10. Father Lord, let our home be devoid of offenses and trouble. Lord Jesus, fill our home with blessings, riches, wisdom, sincerity, humility, understanding, and peace always, in Jesus' mighty name.

11. Father God, I ask that You make us fruitful in the fruit of our body, in Jesus' name. We receive godly seed/children from the throne of grace, in Jesus' name. Our children shall be mighty upon the earth, in Jesus' name.

12. Lord Jesus, let no one desire or contest whatever belongs to me (wife/husband), in Jesus' name. Therefore, in the name that is above all other names, Jesus Christ, I take authority over all activities of anti-marriage demons of incubus and succubus/ Asmodeus (spirit husband/spirit wife) working against my marriage/family, in Jesus' name.

13. In the mighty name of Jesus, I declare that my body is the temple of the Holy Spirit, and every sexual demon that violates/defiles my body is brought under the judgment of God, in Jesus' name (1 Cor. 1:16–17). No weapon formed against my marriage and spouse shall prosper, in Jesus' name.

14. I come against every spirit responsible for divorce, confusion, conflicts, barrenness, infertility, infirmities, unfounded accusation, infidelity, sudden death, lack, and poverty in my marriage, in Jesus' name. I release the fire of God's judgment on all monitoring spirits, mind-binding and mind-blinding demons assigned against my marriage and spouse, in Jesus' name. Whatever evil the powers of darkness have determined against our/my marriage/family shall not come to pass, in Jesus' mighty name (Lk. 22:22).

15. Father Lord, strengthen me against dealing treacherously against the wife of my youth, in Jesus' name (Mal. 2:15). Help us Lord to continue to show deep affection/love for each other, for love covers a multitude of sins. May our love continue to grow for each other every day, in Jesus' name. I reject uncontrollable anger in our lives, in Jesus' name. We shall not give place to the devil in our lives/homes, in Jesus' name (Eph. 4:27).

16. As the Lord lives, we shall build houses and inhabit them; we shall plant vineyards and eat the fruit thereof, in Jesus' name. We shall not build and another inhabit; we shall not plant and another eat. As the days of a tree so shall be our days, and we shall long enjoy the fruits of our labor/hands. We shall not labor in vain nor bring forth for trouble. We are blessed by the Lord so are our children, in Jesus' name (Isa. 65:21–23).

17. Father Lord, I take authority over every wind of afflictions, sea of afflictions, turbulence, and contrary winds that disrupt marriages, in Jesus' name. I stop the operations of these evil forces in my marriage, in Jesus' name. I speak the peace of God over my marriage, in Jesus' name.

18. Father God, I obtain the judgment of the consuming fire against satanic altars, family idols, generational curses, demonic incensing, divination/enchantment, ancestral spirits, foundational

idols of my father's/mother's/spouse's family, serpentine spirits, water spirits, marine spirits/altars, spirit husband/wife, envious witchcraft, household witchcraft, demonic masquerades, demonic dreams, lying spirits, jinx, ancestral curses, necromancy, spells, and sorcery operations that war against marriages and homes that are responsible for instability, barrenness, miscarriages, delayed conception, stillbirth, poverty, laziness, greed, sickness, loss of job/income, misunderstanding, strife, malice, unforgiveness, hatred, divorce, and premature death of spouses. I stop the operations of these evil forces from working against our lives/home and marriage, in Jesus' name.

19. Father Lord, I come against the spirit of uncontrollable anger, bitterness, malice, and envy in my marriage, in Jesus' name (Eph. 4:31–32).

20. Father Lord, in the mighty name of Jesus, I reject every negative influence of social media, unfriendly friends, evil neighbors, family members, house helps/maids, and all strangers to the covenant of marriage on our lives and marriage, in Jesus' name. I plead the blood of Jesus against them, and I cancel their influence on our marriage, in Jesus' name.

21. I decree stability, long life, good health, love, joy, and peace of the Holy Ghost into our lives, home, and marriage, in Jesus' mighty name. I declare that wealth and riches shall be in abundance in our house, and our children shall be mighty upon the earth and shall seat around our table, in Jesus' name (Ps. 112:2–3).

22. I receive divine enablement to discharge the affairs of my life/marriage and home with discretion. I shall not lack discretion, and I shall not reject godly counsel for our lives, in Jesus' name (Ps. 112:5).

23. Father God, Lift up Your banner for us, in Jesus' name (Isa. 49:22). May Christ in us remain the hope of Glory till eternity, in Jesus' name (Col. 1:27).

24. May the Good Lord strengthen us with might according to His glorious power so that we remain faithful to our marriage vows, in Jesus' name. Help us to be fruitful in every good work and increase in the knowledge of God, in Jesus' name (Col. 1:10–11).

Prayer for the Fruit of the Womb and Safe Delivery

1. It is written, "And God blessed them, and God said unto them, Be fruitful, and multiply, and replenish the earth, and subdue it" (Gen. 1:28). Father God, I declare the release of fruitfulness upon my wife/daughter, and I cause every embargo and delay in childbearing removed, in Jesus' name.

2. It is written, "There shall nothing cast their young, nor be barren, in the land" (Exod. 23:26). In the mighty name of Jesus, I curse every demon and altar responsible for miscarriages and barrenness, in Jesus' name. I take authority over the serpentine spirit and household witchcraft operations, in Jesus' name. I declare that the baby shall be born in full term, in Jesus' name!

3. It is written, "Thou shall be blessed above all: there shall not be male or female barren among you" (Deut. 7:14). Father God, I take authority over serpentine spirit operations and ancestral curses responsible for barrenness, in Jesus' name. I declare that I shall not be barren, in Jesus' name. I receive male and female as my reward, in Jesus' name.

4. It is written, "Lo, children are an heritage of the Lord: And the fruit of the womb is his reward. As arrows are in the hand of a mighty man; So are children of the youth. Happy is the man that hath his quiver full of them: They shall not be ashamed, but they shall speak with the enemies in the gate" (Ps. 127:3–5). Father God, I receive boys and girls as my reward from you, in Jesus' name. I declare that my children are God's heritage and shall fulfill their glorious destinies in God and shall be useful for their parents, in Jesus' name. As arrows are in the hand of the mighty, my children shall not miss their targets in the battles of life, in Jesus' name.

5. Father Lord, I ask for Your visitation as you did for Hannah, and she conceived and bore three sons and two daughters, and as you visited Sarah, and she conceived and bare Abraham a son in his old age, at the set time of which God had spoken

to him. Lord, I ask that you visit my wife and daughter and cause her to conceive without stress, in Jesus' mighty name (1 Sam. 2:21; Gen. 21:1–2). I come against every activity of spirit husbands and spirit wives, in Jesus' name.

6. Father God, I receive the inner strength for my wife/daughter to put to bed easily as the Hebrew woman who delivers before the midwives came, in Jesus' name (Exod. 1:19). Lord, make delivery cheap and easy for my wife/daughter, in Jesus' name.

7. It is written, "Before she travailed, she brought forth; before her pain came, she was delivered of a man child. Who hath heard such a thing? Shall the earth be made to bring forth in one day? Or shall a nation be born at once? For as soon as Zion travailed, she brought forth her children. Shall I bring to the birth, and not cause to bring forth? Saith the Lord: shall I cause to bring forth and shut the womb? saith thy God" (Isa. 66:7–9). Father God, I receive easy labor and safe delivery for my wife/daughter, in Jesus' name. I declare there shall be no complications during and after delivery, in Jesus' name!

CHAPTER 7

Praying Parents: Intercession for Children

Praise ye the Lord, Blessed is the man that feared the LORD, that delighted greatly in his commandments. His seed shall be mighty upon the earth: The generation of the upright shall be blessed. Wealth and riches shall be in his house. (Ps. 112:1–2)

Lo, children are an heritage of the Lord, And the fruit of the womb his reward. As arrows are in the hand of mighty man; So are children of the youth. Happy is the man that hath his quiver full of them: they shall not be ashamed,

but they shall speak with the enemies in the gate.
(Ps. 127:3–5)

The children of thy servants shall continue, and their seed shall be established before thee. (Ps. 102:28)

Hear, ye children, the instruction of a father, and attend to know understanding…Let thine heart retain my words: keep my commandments, and live. (Prov. 4:1–4)

Arise, cry out in the night: In the beginning of the watches Pour out thine heart like water Before the face of the Lord: Lift up thy hands toward him for the life of thy young children, that faint for hunger in the top of every street. (Lam. 2:19)

1. Father Lord, I lift up my children to the throne of grace, and I declare that they shall be taught of the Lord, and great shall be my peace over their lives, in Jesus' name. The children You have given me are for signs and wonders. They shall achieve their God's given destiny and no power of hell shall distract them from the path of truth and righteousness, in Jesus' name (Isa. 54:13).

2. Father God, I ask in the name of Jesus that You empower my children not to hear the voice of strangers. Help them to always recognize the voice of the good shepherd and follow the good shepherd, in Jesus' name. Father God, I ask that You cut off every stranger, evil invisible forces, and human agents assigned against their glorious destines, in Jesus' name.

3. Father God, I ask that the power of the Holy Spirit overshadow the lives of my children, in Jesus' name. Let lines fall for them in pleasant places and grant them their godly heritage, in Jesus' mighty name (Ps. 16:6).

4. Father Lord, I ask that You increase my sons and daughters in wisdom and make them of quick understanding and full of the fear of the Lord. May Your love be shed abroad in their hearts by the Holy Ghost, in Jesus' name (Rom. 5:5).

5. Father Lord, I ask that You light their candle and enlighten every darkness around their lives. Let no agent of darkness thrive around their lives. Expose darkness and destroy their operations in their lives, in Jesus' name (Ps. 18:28).

6. Father God, I ask that You teach their hands to war and enlarge their steps under them so that their feet do not slip into sin and darkness, in Jesus' mighty name (Ps. 18:34–36).

7. Dear Lord, I ask that You be their shield, glory, and the lifter up of their heads. Let Your favor locate them all the days of their lives for great opportunities and lifting, in Jesus' name (Ps. 3:3).

8. Dear Lord, let the good hand of God Almighty rest upon their lives, in Jesus' name. Make them a blessing to their generation. Help them to achieve the glorious destiny You have ordained for them, in Jesus' name (Lk. 2:52).

9. Father God, I declare in the name that is above all other names that my children shall be above only and never beneath, in Jesus' mighty name. I ask the Good Lord to make them of quick understanding to be able to discern the negative people with negative influence, in Jesus' name. Empower them Lord to always run away from every appearance of evil, in Jesus' name. Lord, I ask for Your wisdom for them in all things and in all situations. Wisdom is the principal thing in life, give them wisdom and understanding, in Jesus' name (Prov. 4:7).

10. Father Lord, in the mighty name of Jesus, I declare that the rod of the wicked shall not rest upon the destinies of my children, and none of them shall dip their hands into any evil, in Jesus' name (Ps. 125:3).

11. Father Lord, in the name that is above all other names, Jesus Christ, I take authority over every ancestral altar, serpentine altar, household wickedness, familiar spirits, generational curses, and all agenda of the enemy over the destinies of my children. I command them to catch fire now, in Jesus' name.

12. Father Lord, I ask that You deliver my children from strange associations, sexual perversion (lesbians, gay, asexual), falsehood, and all demonic influences prevalent in the world today, in Jesus' name. Teach their hands to war and their fingers to fight. Deliver them from the hurtful sword/arrow of the enemy, in Jesus' name. Be their fortress, high tower, deliverer, and shield. Subdue the powers of darkness under them, in Jesus' mighty name (Ps. 144:1, 2, 7, 10, 11).

13. Lord Jesus, I make a demand upon heaven, and I ask the Good Lord to use my offspring for His glory, in Jesus' name. Lord, make my sons the planting of the Lord and my daughters polished pillars in Your kingdom, in Jesus' name. Let them be relevant in Your program at this end-time, in Jesus' mighty name (Ps. 144:11–12).

14. Father Lord, I ask that in the mighty name of Jesus, all the forces of hell that are set to destroy the tree of my life and its fruits, be arrested, in Jesus' name. I bring upon these forces the vengeance of the Almighty God, in Jesus' name (Jer. 11:19–20).

15. It is written, "And their seed shall be known among the people: all that see them shall acknowledge them, that they are the seed which the Lord hath blessed" (Isa. 61:9). I declare that my children carry God's presence, and they are blessed by the Lord, in Jesus' name. I declare in the mighty name of Jesus that my seed shall be great, and my offspring shall be as the grass of the earth, in Jesus' name (Job 5:25).

16. Father God, I declare that my children shall desire the sincere milk of the word and shall grow by it, in Jesus' name (1 Pet. 2:2). I declare that they shall grow in grace and in the knowledge of our Lord and Savior Jesus Christ, in Jesus' name.

17. I declare that their heads would never lack oil. Lord Jesus, I ask that You open the heavens upon them and pour Your blessing upon them, in Jesus' name. Fill their cup with Your blessings, favor, and riches, in Jesus' mighty name (Ps. 23:5).

18. I declare upon my children that the Almighty God shall be unto them an everlasting light and their glory. A little one shall become a thousand and a small one a strong nation. The Good

Lord will hasten His word to perform it in their lives, in Jesus' name. There shall be no difference between the situation of their lives and the promises of God for their lives, in Jesus' name. Their lives shall be a true reflection of God's promises and glory, in Jesus' name (Isa. 60:19, 22).

19. Father Lord, I ask in the mighty name of Jesus that You pour Your spirit upon my seed and Your blessing upon my offspring. They shall be fruitful and shall take pride in God and make their boast in His holy name (Isa. 44:3–5).

20. Father Lord, I thank You because You are at work in the lives of my sons and daughters both to will and to do Your good pleasure. My sons and daughters are taught of the Lord; they shall not reject the counsel of God for their lives, in Jesus' name (Lk. 7:30). I declare that my children belong to God because they are born of God, and the Holy Spirit lives in them. They are overcomers by the blood of the lamb, in Jesus' name (Rev. 12:11).

21. My sons and daughters shall approve of things that are true, honest, just, pure, and lovely. They shall embrace things that are of good report, full of virtue, and praiseworthy. They shall not be overtaken by the spirit of this end-time and its corruption. My sons and daughters shall tow the godly path, which they have both learned and received in the Lord and great shall be our peace over them, in Jesus' mighty name (Phil. 4:8–9).

22. Lord Jesus, please deliver my sons and daughters from all the activities of dream killers and glory hijackers, in Jesus' name (Gen. 37:5–8). Plant destiny helpers along their path of destinies and compass them about with Your favor, in Jesus' mighty name (Ps. 5:12, Amos 7:5).

23. Father, in the mighty name of Jesus, I come against the fulfillment of every form of negative prophecies, covenants, satanic verdicts, sentences, evil pronouncements, evil wishes, evil imaginations, and demonic utterances from evil altars that may want to influence the destinies of these children negatively, in Jesus' name (Gen. 16:12). I decree every satanic altar, household witchcraft altar, and water spirit altar fighting their destinies catch fire right now, in Jesus' name.

24. Father God, I ask that You empower my children to always delight themselves in the Lord, cause them to ride upon the high places of the earth, and feed them with the heritage of Jacob. Let them feed in large pastures. Bless them with riches and honor. Connect them with rivers in high places, oh Lord, in Jesus' name (Isa. 58:14; 41:18).

25. I declare in the name that is above all names, Jesus Christ that in this season, the Good Lord will keep my children from all the traps of the enemy, and every plan of the enemy to take away their lives prematurely or pervert their destinies is hereby frustrated and terminated, in Jesus' name. The Good Lord shall satisfy them with good health and long life and show them His salvation, in Jesus' name (Job 5:26).

26. Father God, I ask that You empower my children to flee youthful lust and the sexual corruption and perversion that is going on in the world today. Help them to follow righteousness, faith, charity, and peace with them that call upon the name of the Lord out of a pure heart, in Jesus' name (2 Tim. 2:22).

27. Father God, I stand against the prince of air that works in the children of disobedience. I stand against all His operations in the lives of my children, in Jesus' name. My children will not set aside the parental godly teaching, which they have received, in Jesus' name. My children shall be obedient to God and their parents just like the Rechabites in Jeremiah 35:2, 14, 18, 19, in Jesus' name. Lord Jesus, I ask that the fire of the Holy Ghost consume every stranger assigned against their glorious destinies, in Jesus' name.

28. Father Lord, in the mighty name of Jesus, I take authority over the god of this world that blindfolds the minds/eyes of the youth so that the light of God's word does not penetrate their hearts. I stop its operations in the lives of my children, in Jesus' name. I command the light of God's word to shine in their hearts and transform their lives, in Jesus' name (2 Cor. 4:4–6).

29. Father God, light the candle of my children and enlighten every darkness around their lives, in Jesus' name (Ps. 18:28). Let no darkness overtake them as they grow up. Let the power of the

Holy Ghost overshadow them in all seasons of their lives, in Jesus' mighty name. Make them a delightsome land. Make them acceptable to people they come in contact with, in Jesus' name.

30. I reject and I stop every spirit of jealousy, envy, hatred, and discrimination against them, in Jesus' name. Men and women, boys and girls, Black and White/people of color shall compete to favor them everywhere they go at all times, in Jesus' name.

31. Father Lord, I ask that You give them direction in life and order their steps alright into their green pasture and goodly portion, in Jesus' name. May lines fall for them in pleasant places. Lord Jesus, I ask that You take them to places of advantage in life, in Jesus' name (Ps. 16:5–6).

32. Father Lord, I ask that their heavens be opened upon them continuously. Let none of them operate under any close heaven in any area of their lives, in Jesus' name (Matt. 3:16). Lord God, I ask that You be their refuge and their portion in the land of the living, in Jesus' name (Ps. 142:5).

33. May the Good Lord redeem the souls of my children from deceit (deceitful men) and violence (violent men), in Jesus' name. May their blood be precious in the sight of the Almighty God (Ps. 72:14). Lord Jesus, make them the apple of Your eyes, in Jesus' name. I hide them in the blood of Jesus, and I declare that no orchestration of hell against them shall prosper, in Jesus' mighty name.

34. I declare that my children are partakers of God's divine nature. They have the life of Christ in them. I declare that they have the DNA of Jesus Christ. The waster shall not waste them because they are God's anointed and God's prophet, in Jesus' name (2 Pet. 1:3–4; 1 Chron. 16:21–22).

35. Father Lord, I declare that because the earth is the Lord's and the fullness thereof, wherever the sole of the feet of my children shall touch shall be theirs. I declare that my children shall blossom wherever God is planting them and shall eat the good of the land, in Jesus' name (Ps. 24:1; Jos. 1:3, 8).

36. Lord, I ask that You show my children mercy all the days of their lives. Make them candidates of Your mercy everywhere and every day of their lives. Anoint their heads with oil and fill their

cups with Your blessing and favor, in Jesus' name (Rom. 9:15; Ps. 23:5).

37. Father Lord, in the mighty name of Jesus, I activate the ministry of angels in the lives of my children. I mandate their guardian angels to minister protection and preservation for them at all times, in Jesus' name. I ask their guardian angels to open doors of great opportunities for them in life, in Jesus' mighty name.

38. I ask in the mighty name of Jesus that in any matter that pertains to these children, their guardian angels that obey the commands of God will leave no stone unturned, in Jesus' mighty name.

39. May the good hand of the Lord Jehovah be revealed in the lives of all my children in all their endeavors, in Jesus' name (Isa. 66:14).

40. Lord Jesus, I ask that You remove all hindrances/barriers on their pathway, in Jesus' name. Raise a banner for them in all their undertakings, in Jesus' name (Isa. 62:10).

41. Father God, You found David Your servant and with Your holy oil, You anointed him and made him influential. I ask that You anoint my children for greatness. Make my children influential, set their hands upon the sea. Let no power of darkness or any of their agent exact upon their destinies in any way, in Jesus' name (Ps. 89:20–23).

42. Father God, I ask that You empower my children and make them victorious in all battles of life. Let the son of wickedness not afflict them. Beat down their foes before them and plague them that hate them, in Jesus' mighty name (Ps. 89:22–23).

43. Father God, I ask that You deal with them in Your mercy and faithfulness on all issues of their destinies, in Jesus' mighty name. Make Your covenants stand fast with them in every season of their lives, in Jesus' name (Ps. 89:28).

44. Father God, I ask that You exalt their horns like that of the unicorn and cause them to ride in the high places of the earth, in Jesus' name (Ps. 89:24).

45. Father Lord, I ask that Your word be the lamp to their feet and the light to their path all the days of their lives. Let no orchestration of darkness overtake them in the journey of their lives, in Jesus' name (Ps. 119:105).

CHAPTER 8

Divine Healing/Divine Health

Prayer against the spirits of fear, worry, anxiety, evil dreams, demonic oppression, depression, suicide, sleeplessness, sicknesses/infirmities/afflictions, and death

Beloved, I wish above all things that thou mayest prosper and be in health, even as thy soul prospereth. (3 John 1:2)

Heal me, O Lord, and I shall be healed: save me, and I shall be saved: for thou art my praise. (Jer. 17:14)

But he was wounded for our transgressions, he was bruised for our iniquities: the chastisement of our peace was upon him; and with his stripes we are healed. (Isa. 53:5)

Who his own self bare our sins in his own body on the tree, that we, being dead to sins, should live unto righteousness; by whose stripes ye were healed. (1 Pet. 2:24)

Bless the Lord, O my soul, and forget not all his benefits; Who forgives all thine iniquities; who health all thy diseases. (Ps. 103:2–3)

But he answered and said, every plant, which my heavenly Father hath not planted, shall be rooted up. (Matt. 15:13)

But unto you that fear my name shall the Sun of righteousness arise with healing in his wings; and ye shall go forth and grow up as calves of the stall. (Mal. 4:2)

Death and life are in the power of the tongue: and they that love it shall eat the fruit thereof. (Pro. 18:21)

1. **It is written, "Whatsoever I shall bind on earth shall be bound in heaven: and whatsoever I shall loose on earth shall be loosed in heaven." Father Lord, I bind the spirit of sicknesses and infirmity operating in any organ of my body. I lose the hold and grip of these spirits of infirmity from all organs of my body, in Jesus' mighty name (Matt. 18:18).**
2. **It is written, "And ye shall serve the LORD Your God, and he shall bless thy bread, and thy water; and I will take sickness away from the midst of thee" (Exod. 23:25). In the mighty name of Jesus, because I serve the Lord, I declare that I am set free from the curse and trap of sicknesses and infirmities, in Jesus' name.**
3. **Father Lord, I declare that I am empowered to enjoy good health, and that all may go well with me as my soul is pros-**

pering, in Jesus' name. I declare in the mighty name of Jesus that I am delivered from the spirit of sickness, diseases, infirmities, and afflictions, in Jesus' mighty name (3 John 1:2; Ps. 34:19).

4. It is written, "Every plant, which my heavenly Father hath not planted, shall be rooted up" (Mt. 15:13). Father Lord, in the name above all other names, Jesus Christ, the resurrected Lord, I uproot all satanic deposits and plantation from all organs of my body, in Jesus' name.

5. It is written, "But Jesus said unto her, Let the children first be filled: for it is not meet to take the children's bread, and cast it unto the dogs." I declare that because healing is children's meat as being redeemed by the Lord. I declare my healing from all forms of blood sicknesses, diseases, infirmities, and afflictions, in Jesus' name (Mk. 7:27).

6. It is written, "And Jesus stood over her, and rebuked the fever; and it left her: and immediately she arose and ministered unto them." In the mighty name of Jesus, I rebuke high blood pressure, diabetes, cancer, arthritis, barrenness, low sperm count, migraine, heart diseases, and all manner of sicknesses in my body, in Jesus' name. I command You to leave right now, in Jesus' mighty name (Lk. 4:39).

7. I declare that all organs of my body are free from satanic oppression and the effect of the law of death. I declare myself loose from the grip of the spirit of infirmities and sicknesses, in Jesus' name.

8. It is written, "For the law of the Spirit of life in Christ Jesus hath made me free from the law of sin and death" (Rom. 8:2). Therefore, I evoke the law of the spirit of life on all organs of my body, in Jesus' name. I declare that the law of the spirit of life in Christ Jesus is at work in all organs of my body, in Jesus' name. My lungs, kidney, heart, liver, blood, bones, spinal cords, eyes, and brain cells receive the life of God and function normally and effectively now, in Jesus' mighty name.

9. It is written, "But if the Spirit of him that raised up Jesus from the dead dwell in you, he that raised up Christ from the dead shall also quicken your mortal bodies by his Spirit that dwelleth in you" (Rom. 8:11). Therefore, in the mighty name of Jesus, I receive the healing touch of the Holy Spirit to quicken my mortal body out of every sickness, disease, and infirmity in the mighty name of Jesus. I stop every operation of the spirit of death in all organs of my body, in Jesus' mighty name.

10. I come against every spirit of fear, worries, anxiety, and depression, in Jesus' mighty name. I receive the spirit of love, power, and a sound mind, in Jesus' name (1 Tim. 1:7).

11. It is written, "Therefore I say unto you, take no thought for your life, what ye shall eat, or what ye shall drink; nor yet for your body, what ye shall put on, Is not the life more than meat, and the body than raiment? And why take ye thought for raiment? Consider the lilies of the field, how they grow; they toil not, neither do they spin" (Matt. 6:25–33). Lord Jesus, I cast my cares upon You today, and I lay down all my burdens at Your feet, in Jesus' name.

12. I declare that I am free from the hold of fear, worries, anxiety, and mood disorders, in Jesus' name. I free my thoughts, reasoning, and imagination from the satanic influence of fear, worries, sad moods, and anxiety, in Jesus' mighty name.

13. I come against every spirit of suicide, in Jesus' name. I curse and uproot every spirit of suicide, and I stop it from operating in my life and bloodline, in Jesus' name. I reject every foul influence on my thoughts and imagination. I break the grip of suicidal thoughts and ideations on my life, in Jesus' name.

14. I curse the root of the spirit of depression, drug addiction, pornography, lesbianism and homosexuality, and all unclean spirits, in Jesus' name. I stop their operations in my life, in Jesus' mighty name.

15. I curse the root of every spirit of cancer, tumor, high blood pressure, diabetes, low sperm count, and barrenness, in Jesus' name. I stop their operations in my life, in Jesus' name.

16. Father God, I ask in the mighty name of Jesus that Your power be present to always heal me of any ailment, in Jesus' name (Lk. 5:17).

17. I declare that my body is the temple of the Holy Spirit. No sickness or infirmity shall thrive in any organ or cell of my body, in Jesus' name. I decree that any tree that is not yielding any good fruit in my body dry up from its root and be set on fire right now, in Jesus' name (Mk. 11:20).

18. Father God, I ask that You stretch forth Your hand into my life to heal me. Cause me to experience Your supernatural healing touch. Lord, let me experience signs and wonders in my body in the name of Your Holy Child Jesus (Acts 4:30).

19. It is written, "I will ransom them from the power of the grave; I will redeem them from death: O death, I will be thy plagues; O grave, I will be thy destruction: repentance shall be hid from my eyes" (Hos. 13:14). Therefore, I declare and decree in the mighty name of Jesus that without fail, I am delivered from incidents of untimely death and from the power of the grave, in Jesus' name.

20. I declare in the mighty name of Jesus Christ that I have the divine nature of Christ. Sicknesses, diseases, and infirmities have no power over me for I have the life of God in me, and I share the DNA of my Lord Jesus Christ, in Jesus' name.

21. I decree in the mighty name of Jesus that the life of God in me swallow up every death in my body and the glorious light of Jesus in me swallow every darkness around my life, in Jesus' name.

CHAPTER 9

Prayer for Divine Protection against Forces of Darkness

God is our refuge and strength, a very present help in trouble. Therefore, will not we fear, though the earth be removed, and though mountains be carried into the midst of the sea... The Lord of hosts is with us; the God of Jacob is our refuge. (Ps. 46:1–11)

They that trust in the Lord shall be as mount Zion, which cannot be removed, but abideth forever. As the mountains are round about

Jerusalem, so the Lord is round about his people
from henceforth even for ever. (Ps. 125:1–2)

The name of the Lord is a strong tower: the
righteous runneth into it and is safe. (Pro. 18:10)

For I, saith the Lord, will be unto her a wall
of fire round about, and will be the glory in the
midst of her. (Zech. 2:5)

And the Lord will create upon every dwelling place of mount Zion, and upon her assem-
blies, a cloud and smoke by day and the shining
of a flaming fire by night: for upon all the glory
shall be a defence. (Isa. 4:5)

A fire goeth before him, and burnneth up
all his enemies round about. (Ps. 97:3)

1. In the name that is above all other names, I declare that the Lord
   is my keeper. The Lord is my shade upon my right hand. The
   sun shall not smite me by the day nor the moon by night. No
   evil programmed into the sun or the moon shall work against
   me. The Lord shall preserve me from all evil; He shall preserve
   my soul. The Lord shall preserve my going out and coming in
   from this time forth, and even for evermore, in Jesus' name (Ps.
   121:5–8).
2. According to Psalm 91, because I dwell in the secret place of the
   Most High, I shall abide under the shadow of the Almighty, in
   Jesus' name.
3. I declare that the Lord is my refuge and my fortress. I declare
   that no evil shall befall me. I declare that no plague shall come
   near my dwelling, in Jesus' name.
4. The Good Lord shall deliver me from the snare of the wicked
   and from all pestilences raging in the world today. I shall not
   be terrified by the activities of the powers of darkness because

my habitation is in God. I declare that God has empowered His angels to keep watch over my life and all that is mine 24/7, in Jesus' name (Ps. 91).

5. May the Lord make me a fenced brazen wall and my enemies shall fight me, and they shall not prevail against me. For the Lord is with me to save and deliver me (Jer. 15:20). God will deliver me out of the hand of the wicked and will redeem me out of the hand of the terrible, in Jesus' name (Jer. 15:21).

6. Father God, I declare that no enchantment, no divination shall work against my life, family, career, and ministry, in Jesus' name (Numb. 23:23).

7. It is written, "As smoke is driven away, so drive them away: As wax melts before the fire, so let the wicked perish at the presence of God" (Ps. 68:2). I declare that I carry God's presence everywhere I go. I decree that the wicked shall perish in the presence of God in my life, in Jesus' name (Ps. 68:2; Ps. 97:5).

8. Father Lord, I declare that as the wax melts before the fire, let the wicked fighting my destiny perish, in Jesus' name.

9. Father Lord, in the name of Jesus Christ, I activate the ministry of angels for my protection, preservation, deliverance, and the supply of all necessary provisions in my life, in Jesus' name (Ps. 91:11).

10. Father Lord, I ask that You preserve my soul and deliver me out of the hand of the wicked, in Jesus' name (Ps. 97:10).

11. Father Lord, thank You for granting me life and favor. Thy visitation has preserved my life, in Jesus' name (Job: 10:12).

12. It is written, "But the Lord is with me as a mighty terrible one: therefore, my persecutors shall stumble, and they shall not prevail: they shall be greatly ashamed; for they shall not prosper: their everlasting confusion shall never be forgotten," in Jesus' mighty name (Jer. 20:11).

13. I declare that Jehovah has delivered my soul from the hand of evil doers, in Jesus' name (Jer. 20:13).

14. Father God, I declare, "Thou O Lord, art a shield for me; my glory, and the lifter up of mine head," in Jesus' name (Ps. 3:3).

15. It is written, "For the oppression of the poor, for the sighing of the needy, now will I arise, saith the Lord; I will set him in safety from him that puffet at him." Father Lord, I ask that You defend me against every demonic and satanic harassment, in Jesus' name. Arise, O Lord, and let all my enemies be scattered, in Jesus' name (Ps. 12:5).

16. Father Lord, I ask that "You hold up my goings in thy paths, that my footsteps slip not,", in Jesus' name (Ps. 17:5).

17. Father Lord, I ask that You "keep me as the apple of the eye, and hide me under the shadow of thy wings, from the wicked that oppress me, from my deadly enemies, who compass me about," in Jesus' name (Ps. 17:8–9).

18. It is written, "For in the time of trouble he shall hide me in His pavilion: in the secret of His tabernacle shall he hide me; he shall set me upon a rock" (Ps. 27:5). Father Lord, I ask that you build a wall of protection around my life and family, in Jesus' name.

19. I make bold to say, "The Lord is my strength and my shield, my heart trusted in him, and I am helped: therefore, my heart greatly rejoiceth; and with my song will I praise him," in Jesus' name (Ps. 28:7).

20. Thank You, Father Lord, by Your favor thou hast made my mountain to stand strong, in Jesus' name (Ps. 30:7).

21. It is written, "For behold, the darkness shall cover the earth, and gross darkness the people: but the Lord shall arise upon thee, and his glory shall be seen upon thee" (Isa. 60:2). Father God, I ask that You remove every veil of darkness/wretchedness over my destiny, in Jesus' name. Lord Jesus, arise in my circumstance. Let Your glory be seen in my life. Show forth Your might and power in my situation always, in Jesus' name.

CHAPTER 10

The Power to Get Wealth The Law of Sowing and Reaping: Tithing and Giving

Prayer for financial breakthrough in times of economic hardship/ recession

> Blessed is the man that trusts in the LORD, and whose hope the LORD is. For he shall be as a tree planted by the waters, and that spreadeth out her roots by the river, and shall not see when heat cometh, but her leaf shall be green; and shall not be careful in the year of drought, neither shall cease from yielding fruit. (Jer. 17:7–8)

The silver is mine, and the gold is mine, saith the Lord of Hosts. (Hag. 2:8)

But thou shall remember the Lord thy God: for it is he that giveth thee power to get wealth, that he may establish his covenant which he swore unto thy fathers, as it is this day. (Deut. 8:18)

The righteous shall flourish like the palm tree: he shall grow like a cedar in Lebanon. (Ps. 92:12)

While the earth remaineth, seedtime, and harvest, and cold and heat, and summer and winter, and day and night shall not cease. (Gen. 8:22)

Then Isaac sowed in that land, and received in the same year an hundredfold: and the Lord blessed him. And the man waxed great, and went forward, and grew until he became very great: For he had possession of flocks, and possession of herds and great store of servants: and the Philistines envied him. (Gen. 26:12–14)

Bring ye all the tithes into the storehouse, that there may be meat in mine house, and prove me now herewith, saith the Lord of hosts, if I will not open you the windows of heaven and pour you out a blessing that there shall not be room enough to receive it. And I will rebuke devourers for your sakes, and he shall not destroy the fruits of your ground; neither shall your vine cast her fruit before the time in the field saith the Lord of hosts. And all nations shall call you blessed: for ye shall be a delightsome land, saith the LORD of hosts. (Mal. 3:8–12)

But this I say, He which sows sparingly shall reap also sparingly: and he which sows bountifully shall also reap bountifully. (2 Cor. 9:6)

God is able to make all grace abound toward you: that ye, always having all sufficiency in all things, may abound to every good work... Now he that ministers seed to the Sower both minister bread for your food, and multiply your seed sown and increase the fruits of your righteousness; Being enrich in everything to all bountifulness, which cause through us thanksgiving to God. (2 Cor. 9:8–11)

1. It is written "And when money failed in the land of Egypt, and in the land of Canaan, all the Egyptians came unto Joseph, and said, Give us bread: for why should we die in thy presence? For the money faileth." Gen.47:15. Father God, I declare that you are my source, provision, and supply even as money and stocks start to fail and the whole earth is heading towards economic recession in Jesus mighty Name. Keep my soul alive in famine and deliver me from starvation in Jesus mighty Name. Keep me and all mine alive in a period of famine, lack, high cost of living and inflation, in Jesus' name (Ps. 33:19).

2. Father Lord, I receive the power to get wealth and to enjoy it, in Jesus' name (Deut.8:18).

3. Father God, I ask that You bless me as I continue in the covenant practices of tithing and giving, in Jesus' mighty name (Mal. 3:7–10).

4. Father Lord, I ask that You grant me access to hidden riches and treasures of darkness as You promised in the scriptures. Grant me and my generation access to supernatural ideas for wealth creation, in Jesus' name (Isa. 45:3).

5. Father Lord, in the name of Jesus Christ, I ask for rain in the time of the latter rain. Lord, I ask that You make bright clouds upon me and give me showers of rain, to every grass (effort) in the field, in Jesus' name (Zach 10:1).

6. In the name that is above all other names, Jesus Christ, the resurrected Lord, I declare that the Lord commands His blessing upon me in my storehouses, and in all that I set my hand to do, and He shall bless me in the land which the Lord my God giveth me, in Jesus' name (Deut. 28:8–13). May the heavens open upon me and may the presence of God come upon my life mightily and command the favor of God to promote me in all areas of my life, in Jesus' name (Gen. 39:1–6).

7. I declare the blessings of God upon my life in the name that is above every other name, Jesus Christ, the Resurrected Lord. I declare that because I trust in the Lord and because Jesus is my only hope, I am a tree planted by the waters, and I spread my roots by the river. As the Lord lives, I shall not see heat, famine, and lack, but my leaves shall be green. I shall not experience drought, dryness, and economic recession. My life shall be fruitful and productive in all seasons, in Jesus' name (Jer. 17:7–8).

8. Father Lord, I ask that You deliver me in six troubles and in seven let no evil touch me. In famine, I ask that You redeem me from death and war situations and from the power of the sword. Lord, enable me to laugh at destruction and famine and empower me not to be afraid of the beastly elements of the earth. Let all elements be at peace with me, in Jesus' mighty name (Job 5:19–24).

9. It is written, "Prepare thy work without, and make it fit for thyself in the field; and afterward build thine house" (Pro. 24:27). Father Lord, I ask for grace to set achievable goals for my life, in Jesus' name. Help me not to live a careless and visionless life, in Jesus' name.

10. It is written, "And the Lord answered me, and said, 'Write the vision, and make it plain upon tables, that he may run that readeth it'" (Hab. 2:2). Father Lord, I ask that You empower me

from above to pursue the vision (business ideas) You have set before me, in Jesus' name.

11. Father Lord, I ask for the rain of Your blessing upon my endeavors, in Jesus' name. Father God, I ask that You make a bright cloud upon my land and cause me to be fruitful and productive in life, in Jesus' name (Zech. 10:1).

12. It is written, "The Lord was with him, and that which he did, the Lord made it to prosper" (Gen. 39:23). Lord Jesus, I pray that You let the evidence of Your presence be tangible in my life. Make my life productive and cause me to prosper in all I lay my hands to do. Let it be visible for all to see so that they can testify that indeed You are with me, in Jesus' mighty name.

13. It is written, "Then Isaac sowed in the land, and received in the same year a hundredfold: and the Lord blessed him" (Gen. 26:12). Father God, I ask for the anointing to sow in the time of famine and to reap abundantly, in Jesus' mighty name.

14. Father God, I ask that You upgrade my life spiritually and financially, in Jesus' name (3 John 1:2).

15. Father Lord, I make demand on the power of the Holy Ghost. Cause me to soar like the eagle over every obstacle and road block before my destiny, in Jesus' name (Isa. 40:31).

16. In the name that is higher than all other names, Jesus Christ the Resurrected Lord, I frustrate every satanic embargo and demonic agenda decreed against my breakthrough. life, family, and ministry, in Jesus' name.

17. Father Lord, I declare that there shall be blessings without signs or signals coming upon my life, in Jesus' name. I declare that there shall be rivers in the desert places of my life. I declare that there shall be grass in my wilderness. I declare that my life, family, and ministry shall experience rain without clouds; there shall be water without rain. Father Lord, I make a demand on the power of the Holy Ghost, and I ask for unexplainable financial favor in this season, in Jesus' name (2 Kings 3:17).

18. Father Lord, I frustrate and terminate the influence of the power of Sanballat and Tobiah working to hinder my breakthrough in every area of my life, family, and ministry, in Jesus' name.

Lord Jesus, I decree that all satanic gang up against my destiny and breakthrough be consumed by fire, in Jesus' name (Neh. 2:19–20).

19. It is written, "The young lions do lack, and suffer hunger: but they that seek the Lord shall not want any good thing" (Ps. 34:10). Father God, I make a demand on the power of the Holy Ghost for the supernatural supply of all my needs for financial breakthrough, in Jesus' name.

20. It is written, "O, fear the Lord, ye his saints: for there is no want to them that fear him" (Ps. 34:9). Father God, I declare in the mighty name of Jesus that I shall never lack God's provision and abundant blessings, in Jesus' name.

21. It is written, "Thus saith the Lord to his anointed, to Cyrus whose right hand I have holden, to subdue nations before him: and I will lose the loins of kings, to open before him the two leaved gates; and the gates shall not be shut; I will go before thee, and make the crooked places straight: I will break in pieces the gates of brass, and cut in sunder the bars of iron" (Isa. 45:1–2). Therefore, in the name of Jesus as the anointed of God, I declare that doors of great financial opportunities are opening unto me, in Jesus' name. I decree that barriers and satanic opposition to my financial breakthrough are demolished, in Jesus' name.

22. Father God, I ask that You make my wealth heavenly relevant and let it not be a waste, in Jesus' name. I come against the activities of the spiritual thieves, moth, and rust, in Jesus' name (Matt. 6:19–20).

23. Father God, I come against all spiritual forces working against my finances, in Jesus' name. I bind and stop the impact of both natural and spiritual tornado, hurricane, flooding, thunderstorms, fire outbreak, and all destructive forces on my property, warehouses, and investments, in Jesus' name (Job 1:13–17).

24. Father God, I take authority over every government/man-made policy that may lead to economic recession, in Jesus' name. I come against every form of economic siege against the wealth of the nations as witnessed in the siege of Samaria, in Jesus' name. I decree that any bill that would make life unbearable for the

people of God shall not sail through, in Jesus' name (2 Kings 6:24–31).

25. It is written, "Thus saith the LORD, thy Redeemer, the Holy One of Israel; I am the LORD thy God which teaches thee to profit, which leadeth thee by the way that thou should go" (Isa. 48:17). Father God, I ask that You teach me to make a profit on all my investments, in Jesus' name. Lord, help me to invest wisely, in Jesus' name.

26. It is written, "Then Elisha said, Hear ye the word of the LORD, Tomorrow about this time shall a measure of fine flour be sold for a shekel, and two measures of barley for a shekel, in the gate of Samaria" (2 Kings 7:1). Lord God Almighty, I ask that You release the prophetic word that would transform my finances and cause a change of story in my life. Lord, let this word light upon me now, in Jesus' name. Let the divine word that would take me from zero to hero come upon me now, in Jesus' name (2 Kings 7:1; Isa. 9:8).

Prayer for Spiritual Breakthrough and Divine Encounter/Direction Ba'al-Perazim, the God of Breakthrough

The breaker is come up before them: they have broken up, and have passed through the gate, and are gone out by it: their king shall pass before them, and the Lord on the head of them. (Micah 2:13)

So, they came up to Ba'al-Perazim; and David smote them there. Then David said, God hath broken in upon mine enemies by mine hand like the breaking forth of waters: therefore, they called the name of that place Ba'al-Perazim. (1 Chron. 14:11)

For the Lord shall rise up as in mount Perazim, he shall be wroth as in the valley of Gib-e-on, that he may do his work, his strange work; and bring to pass his act, his strange act. (Isa. 28:21)

I am crucified with Christ: nevertheless, I live: yet not I, but Christ liveth in me: and the life which I now live in the flesh I live by the faith of the Son of God, who loved me, and gave himself for me. (Gal. 2:20)

1. Oh, Lord, God Almighty! You are the God of breakthrough. Arise in my life and situation today and break forth for me on all sides. Grant me my needed miracle that will turn every captivity around in my life today, in Jesus' mighty name.
2. Father God, You orchestrated the journey of Saul to meet His destiny helper. Lord, strengthen my spiritual perception and divinely connect me with my destiny helpers, in Jesus' name (1 Sam. 9:18–19).
3. Samuel knew Saul immediately after he saw Him. May my destiny helpers recognize me as soon as they see me or hear my name, in Jesus' name.
4. Help me, Lord, to recognize my destiny helpers whenever I meet them, in Jesus' name.

5. I receive access to divine information that will advance my destiny and needed breakthrough, in Jesus' mighty name.

6. Lord Jesus, I ask for the release of my reserved portion in this season, in Jesus' name (1 Sam. 9:23–24).

7. Lord, it is written, "By whom shall Jacob arise? for he is small." Lord Jesus, I ask that You raise up helpers for me who will be willing to help lift me up from my lowly state, in Jesus' name (Amos 7:2, 5).

8. I receive a supernatural shift from the dunghill/poverty to the palace/wealth as You did in the life of Joseph, in Jesus' name.

9. Lord Jesus, Asher was acceptable to people. I ask that You release upon my life the anointing that will make me acceptable to people You have sent to help my life, in Jesus' name (Deut. 33:24, 11 Sam. 5:1–3).

10. Lord Jesus, I ask that You gird me with strength and make my way perfect. Lord, set my hands upon the sea. Make my feet like the hinds' feet and set me upon my high places, in Jesus' name (Ps. 18:32–33).

11. Oh Lord, I know that the way of man is not in himself. It is not in man that walketh to direct His steps. Oh, Lord! Order by step alright. Teach me the way to go and help to profit, in Jesus' name (Jer. 10:23; Ps. 37:23).

12. Father Lord, the blind man was there at the right time for God to do His work. Lord Jesus, let me be at the right place at the right time for You to showcase Your power of miracles through me, in Jesus' name (John 9:6–7). Let the power in the word of God work for me and not against me, in Jesus' name.

13. Lord Jesus, I ask that You open my eyes to divine opportunity like You did for Hagar in Genesis 21:17–19 and John 21:6. Cause me to soar like the eagle over every obstacle and roadblock before my destiny, in Jesus' name (Isa. 40:31).

14. It is written, "And I will bring the blind by a way that they knew not; I will lead them in paths that they have not known I will make darkness light before them, and crooked things straight" (Isa. 42:16). Father Lord, I ask for Your leading and guidance in all matters of my life and destiny, in Jesus' name.

15. Father Lord, I ask that by Your awesome power remove every obstacle on my path of greatness, in Jesus' name. I declare that in the day that my walls are to be built, in that day shall the decree be far removed, in Jesus' name (Micah 7:11).

16. Dear God, it is written in Lamentation 3:35: "God does not turn the right of a man away." Every power assigned against me hindering and denying my breakthrough, I arrest and bind You today, in Jesus' name.

17. It is written, "For as many as are led by the Spirit of God, they are the sons of God" (Rom. 8:14). Therefore, in the name above every other name Jesus Christ, the Resurrected Lord, as a son in the house, I ask, and I receive the leading of the Holy Spirit that will usher me into my desired breakthrough, in Jesus' mighty name.

18. Father Lord, I ask that You enable me to recognize my green pasture. I ask that You empower me to lie down in my green pasture. May I not miss the blessings, situations, places, and people You have prepared for my breakthrough, in Jesus' name (Ps. 23:2).

19. It is written, "Commit thy works unto the Lord, and thy thoughts shall be established." Father God, I commit my yearnings and aspirations to You today; help me achieve my desire for a breakthrough in all areas of my life, in Jesus' name (Prov. 16:3).

20. Father Lord, I ask that You destroy every monitoring spirit and demonic evil eye assigned to lay surveillance against my breakthrough, in Jesus' name.

CHAPTER 12

Breakthrough Prayer for People Living in a Foreign Land

And the LORD appeared unto him, and said, Go not down into Egypt; dwell in the land which I shall tell thee of: sojourn in this land, and I will be with thee, and will bless thee; for unto thee unto thy seed, I will give all these countries. (Gen. 26:3)

1. It is written, "For now the LORD hath made room for us, and we shall be fruitful in the land." (Gen. 26:22). Father God, let no power of darkness contend our blessing in the land, in Jesus' name. Make room for us in the land, in Jesus' name. Lord make

us fruitful in the land, in Jesus' name. Make it our Rehoboth, in Jesus' name.

2. Father God, I ask that You open my eyes to divine opportunities for greatness in the land, in Jesus' name. Lord, cause us to sow in the land and reap a hundredfold, in Jesus' name (Gen. 26:12).

3. It is written, "Behold, I send an Angel before thee, to keep thee in the way, and to bring thee into the place which I have prepared" (Exo. 23:20). Father God, I ask that You send Your angels to lead me out of every danger or evil in the land, in Jesus' name. May I/we dwell in safety in the land, in Jesus' name.

4. Father God, I ask that You assign Your angels to give me direction in the land, in Jesus' name. Lord. I receive angelic leading and ministration, in Jesus' name. Lord, prosper me and grant me favor and good success, in Jesus' name.

5. Father God, I ask that You make the elements (the sun, moon, stars, rain) to favor and cooperate with me, in Jesus' name.

6. Father Lord, I ask that as I/we sojourn in this land, be with me/ us, and keep me/us from evil. Let it not grieve us bless us and our seed. Lord, be with us and make our generation great. Make my/our seed a blessing, in Jesus' name (Gen. 28:14–15). Lord, perform Your good thought concerning me/us and establish our glorious future/destiny in the land, in Jesus' name.

7. It is written, "Have not I commanded thee? Be strong and of good courage; be not afraid, neither be thou dismayed: for the LORD thy God is with thee withersoever thou goest" (Josh. 1:9). May the Good Lord satisfy me/us with favor early, in Jesus' name. Lord, I ask that You cause me/us to possess wherever the sole of our feet shall tread, in Jesus' name. May kings and queens be our nursing father and mother in the land, in Jesus' name.

8. It is written, "And this is the blessing of Judah: and he said, Hear, LORD, the voice of Judah, And bring him unto his people: Let his hands be sufficient for him; And be thou an help to him from his enemies" (Deut. 33:7). Father God, I ask that You hear my/our voice anytime I/we call in the land and bring me/us to our destiny helpers. Let me/us be acceptable to people and not be discriminated against, in Jesus' name. Enable me/us to dip

my/our feet in oil, in Jesus' name. Lord Jesus, empower me/us to eat the fruit of the land, in Jesus' name. Lord, let my/our hands be sufficient for me/us and be thou my/our help against our enemies. In Jesus' name. Lord, help me/us to continue to observe Your word and covenant diligently, in Jesus' name. May I/we continue to be Your ambassador in the land, in Jesus' name.

9. In the mighty name of Jesus, I take authority over the spirit of the land that may want to make life difficult for me/us in the land. I stop the operations of demonic trafficking and networking with altars of my father's house that may want to hinder my life and destiny in this foreign land, in Jesus' name. Lord, deliver me/us from the evil/violence prevalent in the land, in Jesus' name. Lord, preserve our body, soul, and spirit by the blood of Jesus, in Jesus' name.

10. Father Lord, may the eternal God underneath whose everlasting arms I/we have come to seek refuge remove opposition, obstruction, obstacles, and hindrances from my/our pathway in the land, in Jesus' name. Lord, deliver me from the influence of unfriendly friends and wicked and unreasonable people who may want to work against me/us, in Jesus' name. Lord, deliver me/us from the activities of envious witchcraft from home, in Jesus' name.

11. Father Lord, I ask that You deal bountifully with me/us and let people I/we meet show me/us overwhelming kindness in the land to prove that Your presence is with me/us. Enable men and women, great and low, Black and White to be willing to support, help, and bless me/us with their substance, in Jesus' name.

Prayer for Ministries Praying for Your Calling and Soulwinning

1. Father Lord, I ask that You open the door of utterance for me to speak the mystery of Christ to the body of Christ and to the lost souls to which I am called, in Jesus' name (Col. 4:3).
2. Father, in the name of Jesus, help me, Lord, to take heed to the ministry, which I have received in the Lord, and help me to fulfill it, in Jesus' name (Col. 4:17).
3. Father Lord, help me to stand perfect and complete in all the will of God. Help me to finish well and strong in the Lord, in Jesus' name (Col. 4:12).

4. In the mighty name of Jesus, I obtain the help of God for the fulfillment of my ministry, in Jesus' name (Acts 26:22).

5. Father Lord, grant me the grace, unction, passion, and resources (human/financial) that I need to fulfill my ministry and kingdom work, in Jesus' name.

6. Lord Jesus, I come against any lying/deceiving spirit that may want to deceive/seduce me out of God's purpose and Your good plans for my life and calling, in Jesus' name (2 Chron. 18:21).

7. Father Lord, help me not to neglect the gift of God in my life. Help me to give the needed attention and nurturing to Your gift in my life, in Jesus' name.

8. Dear Lord, make me a blessing to my generation, in Jesus' name. May the gift of God bring profit to me, in Jesus' name (1 Tim. 4:14–15).

9. Father Lord, help me not to be careless about my calling, in Jesus' name (1 Tim. 4:16). As a minister, help me to fulfill the word of God and the mystery of the riches of His glory. May Christ remain the hope of glory in my life, in Jesus' name (Col. 1:25–27).

10. In the mighty name of Jesus, I receive the spirit of godliness and contentment, which is of great gain, in Jesus' name. I take authority over the spirit of worldly lust and covetousness, in Jesus' name (1 Tim. 6:6). I shall not make a shipwreck of my faith and calling, in Jesus' name.

11. Lord Jesus, empower me to walk worthy of God who has called me into His kingdom and glory, in Jesus' mighty name (2 Thes. 1:12). May I be counted worthy of this calling, in Jesus' mighty name.

12. Lord Jesus, I ask that You help me to fulfill all the good pleasure of Your goodness and the work of faith with power. May the name of our Lord Jesus Christ be glorified in me, in Jesus' name (2 Thes. 1:11–12).

13. May the Good Lord make me increase and abound in love toward all men. May the Lord establish my heart unblameable in holiness before God our Father and our Lord Jesus Christ, in Jesus' mighty name (1 Thes. 3:12–13 KJV).

14. Father God, I declare that the word of Christ shall dwell in me richly in all wisdom, teaching, and admonishing people in psalms and hymns and spiritual songs. May my heart be filled with grace, and whatever I do, let it bring glory and thanksgiving to You Lord, in Jesus' name (Col. 3:16–17).

15. Father Lord, in the mighty name of Jesus, I receive the anointing to teach Your word with authority and power, in Jesus' mighty name (Matt. 7:29).

16. Father Lord, help me by Your Spirit not to sin against the Holy Ghost in any area of my life, in Jesus' name (Mk. 3:28–29). Keep me away from sharing Your glory with You as You stretch forth Your hand to do signs and wonders, in Jesus' name.

17. Father Lord, in the name of Jesus, I receive the key to the kingdom, whatsoever I bind on earth, let it be bound in heaven. Whatsoever I lose on earth, let it be loosed in heaven, in Jesus' mighty name (Matt. 18:18).

18. Father Lord, in the mighty name of Jesus, our Resurrected Lord, I receive the anointing to be a fisher of men for Christ, in Jesus' name (Matt. 4:19).

19. Lord Jesus, I ask for the grace to finish strong and well, in Jesus' name. Lord Jesus, I yield my spirit, soul, and body to You. I declare that I shall not lack divine revelation and divine visions. Lord Jesus, empower my mouth with Your word that is quick, powerful, and sharper than any two-edged sword that whatever I bind shall be bound, and whatever I lose shall be loosed, in Jesus' mighty name (Heb. 4:12).

20. Father God, I ask for the grace and power to continue to seek first the kingdom of God and His righteousness in all things. Help me, Lord, to prioritize concerns of the kingdom of God at all times. Help me to consider the agenda of heaven first in all matters, in Jesus' name (Matt. 6:33).

21. Father God, I ask that the power of the Holy Ghost overshadow my life always as I go about declaring the mysteries of Your kingdom, in Jesus' name (Matt. 17:5).

22. Father God, I ask for the grace to forgive at all times those who offend me in the course of the discharge of my ministerial calling, in Jesus' name (Matt. 5:39).

23. Father Lord, I ask that You empower me to be a worthy laborer in Your vineyard, in Jesus' precious name. Give me a burden and the compassion needed to always go after the lost souls, in Jesus' name (Matt. 9:36–37).

24. Father Lord, I ask that You help me to continue to earnestly contend for the faith that was once delivered to the saints, in Jesus' name (Jude 1:3). Help me, Lord, to discern the common from uncommon and the clean from the unclean, in Jesus' name.

25. It is written, "Then shall the righteous shine forth as the sun in the kingdom of their Father" (Matt. 13:43). Father Lord, let this be my testimony at the end of my race on earth, in Jesus' name. Help me, Lord, not to wreck the ship of faith, in Jesus' name.

CHAPTER 14

Prayers for the Revival in the Nations of the World

And I will overthrow the throne of kingdoms, and I will destroy the strength of the kingdoms of the heathen; and I will overthrow the chariots, and those that ride in them; and the horses and their riders shall come down, every one by the sword of his brother. (Hag. 2:22)

For thus saith the Lord of hosts; Yet once, it is a little while, and I will shake the heavens, and the earth, and the sea, and the dry land; And I will shake all nations, and the desire of all nations shall come: and I will fill this house with glory, saith the Lord of Hosts…The glory of this latter house shall be greater than the former, saith the Lord of hosts: and in this place will I give peace, saith the Lord of hosts. (Hag. 2:6–9)

O Lord, I have heard thy speech, and was afraid: O Lord, revive thy work in the midst of the years, in the midst of the years make know; in wrath remember mercy. (Hab. 3:2)

1. Lord Jesus, I ask that You overthrow the throne of darkness ruling the nations of the world, in Jesus' name (Hag. 2:22).

2. Lord Jesus, I ask that the strength of darkness ruling the nations of the world be destroyed, in Jesus' name.

3. Lord Jesus, I ask that the chariots and the riders of the kingdom of darkness ruling the nations of the world be overthrown, in Jesus' name.

4. Father God, I ask that You cause the horses and their riders to come down by the sword of each other, in the name of Jesus.

5. Father Lord, I ask that anointed men and women, young and old, Black and White that You have chosen as Your army for this end-of-the-world revival be commissioned now, in Jesus' name.

6. Father God, I ask that You shake every man-made institution, structure, and strongholds that have constituted a hindrance to the spread of the gospel and the end-time program of God be shaken out of place, in Jesus' name.

7. Father Lord, I ask that You shake all shakable that the desires of the nations of the world may turn to Your programs on earth right now, in Jesus' name.

8. Father God, I ask that You open the heavens and release Your glory on the nations of the world. Lord Jesus, let the glory of the latter house be greater than the former, in Jesus' name.

9. It is written, "The harvest truly is plenteous, but the laborers are few; Pray ye therefore the Lord of the harvest, that he will send forth laborers in to his harvest" (Matt. 9:37). Father God, I ask that in Your mercy ignite the fire of revival all over the nations of the world now, in Jesus' name. Send committed laborers into the harvest field. Lord, let there be a bumper harvest of souls, in Jesus' name.

10. It is written, "For the earth shall be filled with the knowledge of the glory of the Lord, as the waters cover the sea" (Hab. 2:14). Father Lord, I make demand on Your awesome power and release the knowledge of Your word to both great and small, young and old, Black and White, in all nations of the earth, in Jesus' name. Release the understanding of the time the world is in now and Your agenda so that nations would stop living carelessly in disregard to Your timing and program for the end-time, in Jesus' name.

CHAPTER 15

Prayer of Salvation for Lost Souls

Then will I sprinkle clean water upon you, and ye shall be clean: from all your filthiness, and from all your idols, will I cleanse you. A new heart also will I give you, and a new spirit will I put within you: and I will take away the stony heart out of your flesh, and I will give you a heart of flesh. And I will put my spirit within you, and cause you to walk in my statutes, and ye shall keep my judgments, and do them. (Ezek. 36:25–27)

1. Father Lord, I ask for the salvation of the soul of (…), in Jesus' name.
2. Father Lord, I ask that You remove every spiritual blinder and barrier that hinders…from knowing Christ and from accepting Jesus as Lord and savior, in Jesus' name.
3. Father Lord, I ask for a new heart for (…), in Jesus' name.
4. Father Lord, I ask that You give (…) a new heart, in Jesus' name.
5. Father Lord, I ask that You remove the stony heart out of (…), in Jesus' name.
6. Father Lord, I ask that You give (…) a heart of flesh that will yield to You always, in Jesus' name.
7. Father Lord, I ask that You put Your spirit within (…), in Jesus' name. Make his/her spirit alive in Christ, in Jesus' name.

8. Father Lord, I ask that You empower (…) to walk in Your statues all the days of his life, in Jesus' name.

9. Father Lord, I ask that You enable him/her by Your spirit in his/her inner man to keep Your word in his/her heart and to do them, in Jesus' name.

10. Father Lord, I ask that You shed abroad the love of Christ in his/her heart, in Jesus' name.

11. It is written, "The heart of the King is in the hand of God." Father God, I ask that You turn his/her heart to Christ, in Jesus' name.

12. Father Lord, I ask that You open his/her eyes of understanding to the truth of the love of Christ, in Jesus' name.

13. Father Lord, I ask that You open his/her heart to the love of God, in Jesus' name.

14. Father Lord, I ask that You bring him/her to a state of true repentance, in Jesus' name.

15. Father Lord, I ask that You forgive him/her and cleanse him/her with the blood of Jesus that was shed at Calvary, in Jesus' name.

16. Father God, I receive the abundant life in Christ Jesus for him/her, in Jesus' name.

17. Father God, I ask that You put eternity in his/her heart, in Jesus' name.

18. Father God, I ask that the great helper, the Holy Spirit teach him/her all things that pertain to life in Christ and godliness, in Jesus' name.

19. Father God, I ask that You give him/her the mind of Christ and a humble heart, in Jesus' name.

20. Father Lord, I ask that You keep and bless him and make Your face to shine upon him/her, in Jesus' name.

Be Wise Now! Run for Your Dear Life

The conies are but a feeble folk; yet make
their houses in the rock. (Prov. 30:26)

The high hills are a refuge for the wild goats
and the rocks are for the conies. (Ps. 104:18)

Conies are quite vulnerable and are of little stature and strength. They are very fragile and tender-looking. They live in the bush under the cleft of the rocks for their safety and survival from ferocious animals like lions, leopards, and tigers.

However, as vulnerable as the conies seem to be, they are a rare breed of great wisdom who have sufficient wisdom to seek protection under the cleft of the rock. If lesser animals have sufficient wisdom to seek protection under the cleft of the rock, in the face of seeming danger, it behooves man that is of a higher breed of God's creation to seek protection and salvation in the rock of all ages, Jesus Christ.

The world today is negatively skewed. The scriptures described the world you and I live in as the habitation of cruelty/wickedness. The devil is out in the world fulfilling his mission of stealing, killing, and destroying humanity through lust, corruption, sicknesses, afflictions, demonic attacks, and sinful lifestyles.

And There Was No Room in the Inn

Remember, Jesus was born in a manger because there was no room in the inn. Would you give Him room in your heart? Give Jesus a room in your heart today. Jesus has come to give us life and life in abundance. All other gods are thieves, murderers, and destroyers. Come to Jesus today. He will never cast you out. If you place your faith in Jesus Christ today, asking Him to forgive you of all your sins, He will cleanse you with His blood, which He shed for the world on the cross of Calvary. He will forgive you and also write your name in the Book of Life. Jesus Christ, our savior, will accept you as His own and will save you from the burning hell reserved for sinners.

Be wise now! Run to Jesus today for the salvation of your precious soul!

Sinners' Prayer

Dear Lord Jesus, I am sorry for all my sinful lifestyles. I believe You died for me on the cross of Calvary. Please forgive me and cleanse me from all my sins by Your blood that was shed for me at Calvary. Thank You for accepting me in the beloved. Thank You for writing my name in the Book of Life. Thank You for the gift of eternal life. I place my faith in You today. I accept and acknowledge You as my Lord and savior. Give me power to live above sin so that the devil would not have any hold over my life. Thank You, Lord, for saving my soul, in Jesus' name.

Hymns/Songs

In Christ alone my hope is found
He is my light, my strength, my song
This cornerstone, this solid ground
Firm through the forest drought and storm
What heights of love, What depths of peace
When fears are stilled, when strivings cease
My comforter, my all in all
Here in the love of Christ I stand

In Christ alone who took on flesh
Fullness of God in helpless babe
This gift of love and righteousness
Scorned by the ones He came to save
Till on that cross as Jesus died
The wrath of God was satisfied
For every sin on Him was laid
Here in the death of Christ I live
There in the ground His body lay

Light of the world by darkness slain
Then bursting forth in glorious day
Up from the grave He rose again
And as He stands in victory
Sin's curse has lost its grip on me
For I am His and He is mine
Bought with the precious blood of Christ

No guilt in life, no fear in death
This is the power of Christ in me
Life's first cry to final breath

Jesus commands my destiny
No power of hell, no scheme of man
Can ever pluck me from His hand
Till He returns or calls me home
Here in the power of Christ I'll stand

By Stuart Townsend

Confession of Faith

When men are saying there is a casting down for them, I shall say the Lord my God has lifted me up. I am lifted and made to sit with Christ in the heavenly places far above all principality and power and might and dominion and every name that is named, not only in this world but also in that which is to come (Job 22:29; Eph. 1:20–21).

About the Author

Kehinde Adelusi is an ordained minister who shares the truth of God's word in various church settings and crusades. She is a pastor's wife, a praying mother, and a prayer warrior. She is also an educationist, a professional counselor, and a public speaker.

www.ingramcontent.com/pod-product-compliance
Lightning Source LLC
Chambersburg PA
CBHW020628160726
47991CB00002B/954